German Radioactive Waste

This book presents the universal issue of radioactive waste management from the perspective of the German legal system, analysing how lawmakers have responded to the problem of nuclear waste over the course of the last 70 years.

In this book, Robert Rybski unwraps and explains the perplexing legal and social issues related to radioactive waste. He takes readers through the entire "life-cycle" of radioactive waste: from the moment that radioactive material is classified as radioactive waste, through the period of interim storage, and right up to its final disposal. However, this last step in radioactive waste management (that of final disposal) has not yet been achieved in Germany, or anywhere in the world, and has been the subject of hefty public debate for dozens of years. As a result, the book analyses the most recent regulations in place to enable final disposal.

This book will be of interest to energy policy experts, academics and professionals who work in the area of nuclear energy.

Robert Rybski is Assistant Professor working at the Faculty of Law and Administration, University of Warsaw, Poland. He is also Chief Specialist in the Financial Market Development Department at the Polish Financial Supervision Authority (KNF), and previously worked as a lawyer specialising in climate and energy law for ClientEarth. For voluntary work, he acts as University of Warsaw Rector's Plenipotentiary for Environment and Sustainable Development.

Routledge Focus on Environment and Sustainability

Learning to Live with Climate Change
From Anxiety to Transformation
Blanche Verlie

Social Innovation in the Service of Social and Ecological Transformation
The Rise of the Enabling State
Olivier De Schutter and Tom Dedeurwaerdere

Gender, Food and COVID-19
Global Stories of Harm and Hope
Edited by Paige Castellanos, Carolyn E. Sachs and Ann R. Tickamyer

Natural Resource Leadership and Management
A Practical Guide for Professionals
Frederick Cubbage

Monetary Policy and Food Inflation in Emerging and Developing Economies
Abdul-Aziz Iddrisu and Imhotep Paul Alagidede

Mathematical Models and Environmental Change
Case Studies in Long Term Management
Douglas J. Crookes

German Radioactive Waste
Changes in Policy and Law
Robert Rybski

For more information about this series, please visit: www.routledge.com/Routledge-Focus-on-Environment-and-Sustainability/book-series/RFES

German Radioactive Waste

Changes in Policy and Law

Robert Rybski

LONDON AND NEW YORK

First published 2022
by Routledge
4 Park Square, Milton Park, Abingdon, Oxon OX14 4RN

and by Routledge
605 Third Avenue, New York, NY 10158

Routledge is an imprint of the Taylor & Francis Group, an informa business

British Library Cataloguing-in-Publication Data
A catalogue record for this book is available from the British Library

Library of Congress Cataloging-in-Publication Data
A catalog record for this book has been requested

ISBN: 978-1-032-05506-0 (hbk)
ISBN: 978-1-032-06504-5 (pbk)
ISBN: 978-1-003-19808-6 (ebk)

DOI: 10.4324/9781003198086

Typeset in Times New Roman
by Apex CoVantage, LLC

Contents

Acknowledgments

First of all, I would like to express my thanks to the promoter of my doctoral thesis, prof. dr habil. Marek Zubik – especially for the already 14 years of supporting my research development as well as for enormous effort in motivating and supervising my doctoral thesis. Also this superb subject and title of my PhD – "Constitutional aspects of nuclear energy in the jurisprudence of the Federal Constitutional Court and in theses of German constitutional law doctrine" – were an inspiration from prof. dr habil. Marek Zubik.

Preparation of the doctoral thesis was preceded by a master's degree at the Law Faculty of the Humboldt-Universität zu Berlin, where I defended my master thesis under the following title: "Constitutional Aspects of the Nuclear Energy in Germany. Models of an Entry and of an Exit" (original: "Verfassungsrechtliche Aspekte der Kernenergie in Deutschland. Modelle des Ein- und Ausstiegs"). Thus I would like to express my gratitude also to the promoter of master thesis – Mr Prof. Dr. Marcus Schladebach – for his kind consent to become a promoter on this socially difficult subject in Germany and for all of his efforts and support. Defending a master thesis (38 pages long) at a German university under a concurrent title enabled me to precisely develop a structure of the future doctoral thesis as well as to identify key issues that were then analysed in the doctoral thesis (444 pages long).

My doctoral thesis was prepared during 6 years of doctoral studies at the Faculty of Law and Administration of the University of Warsaw and I would like to express my gratitude towards all the administrative staff that supported me a lot, especially our librarians.

Simultaneously I would like to thank reviewers of my doctoral thesis – to Mr prof. dr habil. Leon Kieres and to Mr prof. dr habil. Andrzej Wróbel and to blind peer-reviewers of the proposal for this book for their valuable suggestions.

For financial support in publishing this book in an open access standard, I would like to thank prof. dr habil. Tomasz Giaro, Dean of the Faculty of Law and Administration of the Warsaw University.

Finally, I would like to thank for the immense help in publishing this book Adrian Warsiński, dr habil. Maciej M. Sokołowski and Honorable Stephen G. Burns.

Acronyms and abbreviations

Atomic Law	Federal Act of 23 December 1959 on the Peaceful Utilisation of Atomic Energy and the Protection against its Hazards (*Atomgesetz*)
BASE	Federal Office for the Safety of Nuclear Waste Management (*Bundesamt für die Sicherheit der nuklearen Entsorgung)*
BGB	German Civil Code (*Bürgerliches Gesetzbuch*)
BGBl	Public gazette of the Federal Republic of Germany (*Bundesgesetzblatt*)
BGE	State-owned company responsible for i.a. site selection procedure (*Bundesgesellschaft für Endlagerung*)
BMU	Federal Ministry for the Environment and Reactor Safety (*Bundesministerium für Umwelt, Naturschutz und nukleare Sicherheit*)
BVerfGE	An abbreviation for the official gazette that publishes judgments and some of the rulings of the German Federal Constitutional Court in Karlsruhe (*Bundesverfassungsgerichts-Entscheidungen*)
BVerfGE 104, 238, p. 239.	Within this book I copy the manner of referring to particular fragments of judgments of the FCC as it is the manner within the German constitutional law doctrine of how the FCC does that. The first number stands for the volume of BVerfGE in which that particular judgment was published. The second number stands for the first page in that particular volume on which that judgment is printed. The third number refers to a particular fragment

	of a judgment (in a way that was published in BVerfGE).
FCC	German Federal Constitutional Court in Karlsruhe (*Bundesverfassungsgericht*)
HLRWD-Commission	High-Level Radioactive Waste Disposal Commission (*Kommission Lagerung hoch radioaktiver Abfallstoffe*)
NJW	German journal *Neue Juristische Wochenzeitung*
NVwZ	German journal *Neue Zeitschrift für Verwaltungsrecht*
Standortauswahlgesetz	Federal Act of 23 July 2013 on searching and selecting the location of a radioactive waste disposal facility (commonly known as: *Standortauswahlgesetz)*
Strahlenschutzverordnung	Radiation Protection Ordinance
SZL	Interim storage facility for radioactive waste located at a nuclear power plant (*Standortzwischenlager*)
ZUR	German journal *Zeitschrift für Umweltrecht*

Glossary

Atomausstieg I Nuclear phase-out agreement from 2001

Atomausstieg II Nuclear phase-out decision from 2011

Basic Law The German Constitution (*Grundgesetz*)

Bundestag Lower chamber of the German Parliament

Bundesrat Higher chamber of the German Parliament

Deutschmarks German currency that was substituted with Euro

Disposal facility Any facility or installation the primary purpose of which is radioactive waste disposal. Its aim is to permanently seal radioactive waste from the environment

Energiewende A process that mirrors *Atomausstieg I.* It is a phase-out of all fossil fuels (including uranium and plutonium) in Germany. It started with the *Atomausstieg I* as a way to transform the German energy system.

Atomic Law Federal German Atomic Energy Act (*Atomgesetz*)

German Democratic Republic Eastern Germany. In 1990 it was reunified with the Federal Republic of Germany

Grundgesetz The German Constitution

Land One of the 16 federal states in Germany

Länder Federal states within the constitutional system of the Federal Republic of Germany

Laufzeitverlängerung Political decision from 2010 to modify *Atomausstieg I* and to prolong operating of commercial nuclear reactors in Germany

MP Member of the German Parliament

Spent fuel nuclear fuel that has been irradiated and permanently removed from a reactor core

Introduction

The book presents the universal issues of high-level radioactive waste management from the perspective of the German legal system. It covers the entire "life-cycle" of radioactive waste, i.e. from the moment that radioactive material is classified as radioactive waste (Chapter 1), through the period of interim storage (Chapter 2), up to its final disposal (Chapter 3). But this final step in radioactive waste management (final disposal) has not yet been achieved in Germany (or anywhere in the world). It was the subject of a hefty public debate in Germany for dozens of years. Thus the book analyses in a separate chapter (No. 3) the most recent regulations that are to enable radioactive waste disposal. This framework is a result of public consensus. The book also analyses another controversial issue of re-using spent nuclear fuel. For decades, this concept of closing the nuclear fuel cycle was supported by the German lawmaker until it came to an abrupt halt. The timeframe for this comprehensive depiction of regulatory developments in the area of radioactive waste management in Germany starts with the emergence of the nuclear power sector in Germany up until most recent regulatory developments (after statutory shut-down).

The central research objective of this book was to analyse how private and public entities bear both responsibility and liability within the process of nuclear waste management. On one hand it is a clear constitutional task of the state to protect the life and health of its citizens as well as to protect the environment. But on the other hand, should the taxpayer be involved in financing those tasks if the (private) polluters are well-known? The well-established "polluter-pays" principle finds its application in this area only partially as the long-term risks (that go far into the future for dozens of generations) complicate undertaking any calculations regarding the costs of final disposal of radioactive waste. The other problem is whether those private entities will still exist once exact calculations are finalised. The book presents and assesses an approach taken by a German lawmaker while trying to get out of this *zugzwang*.

DOI: 10.4324/9781003198086-1

Although the book focuses solely on the German legal system, problems described in it are present in other legal systems. Could those universal problems be solved using the German experience? I personally believe so because the German approach to the nuclear waste issue is a leading one in the world. The current German regulatory framework is a result of decades of hefty public and legal debate. Although those regulations might not be perfect, it is a bold attempt to address these issues by the generations that used nuclear power (and not to leave this problem to future generations). At the same time, other countries that use nuclear energy have not had a similarly vivid public and/or legal debate on radioactive waste management. Thus, even if their legal systems were to now address the issues of final management of radioactive waste, at some point in the future these measures may lack public support. Thanks to identifying these three stages of regulatory responses, readers outside Germany will be able to easily identify the stage to which their own legal system can be assigned.

1 The nuclear energy sector and its by-products

The most topical issue concerning the nuclear energy sector in the present-day Germany is the management and treatment of radioactive waste. When deciding to make peaceful use of nuclear energy in 1959, the statutory lawmaker did not establish any regulation dealing with radioactive waste,[1] even underestimated it.[2] The amount of the generated radioactive waste has been increasing each year since Germany started making practical use of nuclear technology. Meanwhile, managing and treating nuclear waste is not an easy task. The earliest regulations addressing the matter of nuclear waste were adopted only in 1976.[3] When it comes to nuclear waste management, Germany is still looking for the right solution, and this concerns both theoretical – legal solutions and practice.

Radioactive waste is a by-product of the process of generation of electricity in nuclear power plants, in the course of dismantling of the decommissioned nuclear installations, during research and development activities, in medicine and industry.[4] We can speak of low-level, intermediate-level and high-level radioactive waste. Another classification divides radioactive waste into: heat generating radioactive waste (high-level and some intermediate-level waste) and low heat generating waste (low-level and most intermediate-level waste).[5] Radioactive waste can also be divided according to how long radioactive radiation exceeds the permissible levels. Hence the division of radioactive waste into: "short-lived waste" with a lifespan of under 300 years, and "long-lived waste" whose lifespan (i.e. full decomposition period) is significantly greater than 300 years, amounting possibly to millions of years.[6] Most of the high-level radioactive waste in Germany includes spent fuel and vitrified waste coming from facilities that process spent fuel.[7] It is estimated that the amount of low- and intermediate-level radioactive waste in Germany will reach approximately 227,000 cubic metres by 2040.[8] As for the amount of high-level waste (until the decommissioning of nuclear power plants), it is said to reach approximately 29,000 cubic metres.[9]

DOI: 10.4324/9781003198086-2

The issues related to radioactive waste, apart from the physical management of such waste, focus also on the assurance of protection against radioactive radiation, whose sources may include both radioactive waste and other radioactive material earmarked for further use. On account of the occurrence of ionising radiation, every kind of radioactive material is a potential threat to the health and life of humans and the natural environment.[10] Such threats result from wrong (incompetent) utilisation of such radioactive material or from using it not as intended.[11] The main issue in this context is the state's duty to dispose of radioactive waste in an organised manner, which is an initiative that is in the interest of all German citizens.[12] Another important aspect is the cost of disposal of radioactive waste and the determination of the entity to bear this cost.[13] Interestingly, finding a solution for radioactive waste may result in increasing public acceptance towards nuclear energy.[14]

1. The concept of radioactive waste

First of all, it is necessary to determine the meaning of the notion of "radioactive waste". According to encyclopaedic knowledge, it is

> objects or materials (in different states of matter) contaminated with radioactive substances to an extent exceeding the limits permitted under the adopted and binding regulations, and not earmarked for further use. Radioactive waste is generated anywhere where radioactive substances are utilised – at uranium processing plants, in nuclear reactors; it is also produced in processes involving the use of radioactive isotopes in the field of engineering, medicine, biology, agriculture, etc.; highest-level radioactive waste is a product of the nuclear energy sector.[15]

According to the existing judicial decisions, radioactive waste is radioactive material that needs to be neutralised and isolated from the natural environment if it can be characterised by any of the following criteria: 1) the current state of the art does not make it possible to process the radioactive material safely; 2) it would not be feasible to safely reuse such radioactive material; 3) it would be impossible to reconcile the use of the radioactive material with the protection objectives described in §1 items 2–4 of Atomic Law.[16] According to the safeguard provisions referred to in this ruling, it is necessary to first protect the life and health of people against the hazards posed by nuclear energy and the harmful impact of ionising radiation (§1 item 2). All initiatives intended to deal with waste should aim to prevent danger to the internal or external security of the Federal Republic of Germany from the application or release of nuclear energy or ionising radiation (§1 item 3).

Speaking in general terms, the adopted manner of dealing with radioactive waste needs to enable the Federal Republic of Germany to meet its international obligations in the field of nuclear energy and radiation protection (§1 item 4). At the same time, the obligation to abide by the protection standard provided for in the cited provisions of Atomic Law is imposed on anyone who builds and operates or manages a nuclear installation, or significantly converts, stops, or cleans an installation which processes nuclear fuel, and engages in initiatives involving dealing with radioactive material or adapts the installation to the generation of ionising radiation.

The definition of radioactive waste stems also directly from Germany's federal legislation. The *Strahlenschutzverordnung* ordinance (Radiation Protection Ordinance) of 20 July 2001[17] defined radioactive waste in §3 para. (2) item 1 letter a) as radioactive substances pursuant to §2 para. (1) of Atomic Law, which, according to §9a of Atomic Law, are to be disposed of in a regulated manner.

It is also important to see the difference between radioactive waste and such radioactive substances which will not be classified as radioactive waste on account of their low radioactivity. Pursuant to §3 para. (2) item 1 letter a) *in fine* of the *Strahlenschutzverordnung* ordinance of 20 July 2001, the discharges that do not exceed the radioactivity levels pursuant to §47 of the ordinance are not considered radioactive waste. According to §47 para (1) of the *Strahlenschutzverordnung* ordinance, in the case of the planning, construction, operation, decommissioning, safe enclosure and dismantling of facilities or installations, an individual member of the general public may be exposed to water-borne or air-borne radiation generated by said facilities or installations at the level of 0.3 mSv per calendar year. This radiation level pertains to the impact on the entire organism. Higher levels apply only to some organs (e.g. the lungs – 0.9 mSv, the skin – 1.8 mSv).

In the period when the reprocessing of spent fuel was still permitted and there was a statutory guarantee of precedence on spent fuel management in place, the definition of radioactive waste, in line with the *Strahlenschutzverordnung* ordinance of 20 July 2001, included an element of obligation of determination that it was not safe to reuse such radioactive material.[18] This stemmed from the then-binding statutory guarantee of precedence on spent fuel reprocessing. Moreover, it was necessary to clearly determine whether the spent fuel considered was radioactive material or radioactive waste. According to the existing judicial decisions, even if Germany does not have the necessary installations to reprocess spent fuel, such fuel is still radioactive material and therefore shall not be categorised as radioactive waste.[19] When the reprocessing of spent fuel became prohibited with the adoption of *Atomausstieg I*, the above interpretation of Atomic Law was no longer valid. Spent fuel had been qualified as radioactive material fit for reprocessing until the establishment of *Atomausstieg I*. Now, it is considered radioactive waste.

The moot point is whether radioactively contaminated soil should also be considered radioactive waste within the meaning of Atomic Law and the first *Strahlenschutzverordnung* ordinance issued pursuant to the said act.[20] In the early 1990s, radioactively contaminated soil was categorised like other instances of land contaminated by industrial activity.[21] Such contamination was, however, not covered or addressed by Atomic Law.[22] This legal landscape survived also on the grounds of the *Strahlenschutzverordnung* ordinance of 20 July 2001,[23] but changes within the currently binding *Strahlenschutzverordnung* ordinance of 29 November 2018 are covered in Chapter 3.

2. Constitutional competence for the federation to act within the area of radioactive waste

The level of detail displayed in Germany's Constitution of 1949 may seem surprising. The Constitution (from its 1959 amendment onwards) granted the Federation the right to establish statutory regulations also in the area of radioactive waste. According to Article 73 (1) item 14 of Grundgesetz:

> The Federation shall have exclusive legislative power with respect to: [. . .]
> 14) [. . .] the disposal of radioactive substances.

Such wording of the provisions of the Constitution plays a significant part in the country's federal system. It means that only the Federation has the power to establish legislative regulations regarding the matter in question. Article 73(1) item 14 of Grundgesetz gives the Federation the constitutional grounds to handle this matter at all in the first place. The federal legislator does not have to act in collaboration with any other authority here.[24] Moreover, the fact that the Constitution makes this competence an exclusive legislative power of the Federation rules out the legislative activity of Länder in this area.[25] But it does not make it impossible for the federal legislator to clearly and expressly authorise the federal states to act.[26] This is provided for in Article 71 of the Constitution: "On matters within the exclusive legislative power of the Federation, the Länder shall have power to legislate only when and to the extent that they are expressly authorised to do so by a federal law".

The provisions of Article 73(1) 1 item 14 of *Grundgesetz* refer to the disposal of "radioactive substances" (*radioaktiver Stoffe*). The definition of radioactive waste, used in the relevant legislation,[27] makes use of the notion of "radioactive substances" (also referred to as "radioactive material") as well. It is therefore necessary to first determine what the "radioactive substances" referred to in Article 73(1) item 14 means. In particular, it is important to establish whether the commonly used notion of radioactive waste may be considered tantamount to the "disposal of radioactive substances" mentioned in *Grundgesetz*. The Constitution uses a notion from the area of nuclear physics also in this context.[28] First, it may be reasonable to apply one of the two methods proposed in the literature on the subject. These methods involve referring to the encyclopaedic definition, i.e. stemming from biological-natural sciences, and using the definition found in Atomic Law.

One interpretation of the notion of "radioactive substances" is based on the encyclopaedic source. In the light of this interpretation, radioactive substances within the meaning of the said provision include all and any substances that contain radioactive nuclides (radionuclides) or are radioactively contaminated.[29] The term "nuclide" means "an atom defined by a specific number of protons and neutrons found in its nucleus [. . .]; nuclide is often understood as the sole nucleus of such an atom".[30] The radioactivity of nuclides is to pertain to such a quality that makes them change into other nuclei without any external impact, and release kinetic energy in the form of electromagnetic radiation at the same time.[31] The term "radioactivity", in turn, means "emission of nuclear radiation, i.e. of light nuclei or nucleons, leptons, photons, accompanying spontaneous transformations of atomic nuclei".[32]

Another method applied by some authors analysing Article 73(1) item 14 of Grundgesetz when it comes to the notion of "the disposal of radioactive waste" involves references to the definition included in Atomic Law.[33] §2(1) of Atomic Law reads as follows:

> radioactive material (nuclear fuel and other radioactive substances) refers to all material containing one or more radionuclides and whose activity or specific activity in conjunction with nuclear energy or radiation protection cannot be disregarded under the provisions of this Act or a statutory ordinance promulgated on the basis of this Act. The term "nuclear fuel" refers to special fissionable material in the form of:
>
> 1 plutonium 239 and plutonium 241;
> 2 uranium enriched in isotopes 235 or 233;
> 3 any material containing one or more of the substances cited under nos. 1 and 2;
> 4 substances which permit a self-sustaining chain reaction to be maintained in a suitable installation and which are defined in a statutory ordinance.

The said provision of Atomic Law defines radionuclide as an unstable nuclide which undergoes a spontaneous decay without any external factors.[34] It also interprets "activity" as the number of atomic nuclei which decay in a given radioactive substance.[35]

The fact that these two notions (radioactive waste and "the disposal of radioactive substances") are based on the notion of "radioactive substances" or "radioactive material" implies that they should be interchangeable, as seen in the Constitution. Moreover, the purpose underlying these two definitions is identical – the aim is to neutralise any disposable radioactive substances. It should be therefore acknowledged that Article 73(1) item 14 refers exactly to radioactive substances/radioactive material. This way one can acknowledge that the Constitution granted the Federation appropriate legislative power in the domain of radioactive waste.

The constitutional legislator's and statutory lawmaker's areas of interest include also those radioactive substances, which are not subject to statutory regulation for specific reasons. The criteria in this domain are set by §2 para (1) of Atomic Law. The provision of §2 para (2) was incorporated into the text of Atomic Law in relation to the implementation of the Euratom Directive in order to define the criteria providing the grounds for excluding radioactive substances from state regulation (this concerns the determination of the activity or concentration of a given radioactive substance).[36] This matter is particularly important because it involves setting the limits for the permissible release of radioactive substances into the natural environment.[37] Examples include releases of substances from nuclear fuel reprocessing installations into the air.

The quoted statutory definition under §2 para. (1) of Atomic Law referred directly to the solutions included in the Treaty establishing the European Atomic Energy Community (the Euratom Treaty).[38] Article 197 items 1 and 2 of the Euratom Treaty read:

> For the purposes of this Treaty:
>
> 1 "Special fissile materials" means plutonium 239; uranium 233; uranium enriched in uranium 235 or uranium 233; and any substance containing one or more of the foregoing isotopes and such other fissile materials as may be specified by the Council, acting by a qualified majority on a proposal from the Commission; the expression "special fissile materials" does not, however, include source materials.
>
> 2 "Uranium enriched in uranium 235 or uranium 233" means uranium containing uranium 235 or uranium 233 or both in an amount such that the abundance ratio of the sum of these isotopes to isotope 238 is greater than the ratio of isotope 235 to isotope 238 occurring in nature.

The description of a radioactive material as included in §2 para. (1) of Atomic Law differentiates between nuclear fuel as materialisation of different forms of fissile materials and other types of radioactive materials.[39] Meanwhile, "the disposal of radioactive substances" as referred to in Article 73 (1) item 14 of *Grundgesetz* focuses on elimination of hazards posed by radioactive substances.[40] This encompasses all and any means to neutralise radioactive substances.[41] This means therefore that the constitutional interpretation is much broader. Atomic Law concentrates on fission of nuclear fuel in nuclear reactors in appropriate conditions (which leads to reducing the radioactivity of nuclear fuel due to the release of kinetic energy from it). Apart from the argument based on physical processes, referring the statutory notion to the Constitution is wrong also on account of the special, i.e. supreme, legal rank of the Constitution in the German system of commonly applicable sources of law. Adopting such an approach would lead to questioning the hierarchical structure of the system of the sources of law. For this reason, the said manner of interpretation of *Grundgesetz* should be rejected. But one should not ignore the outcomes of historical interpretation when it comes to the interpretation of the provisions of *Grundgesetz*. The Constitution's provisions pertaining to nuclear energy were incorporated on account of Germany's accession to Euratom. This means, however, a need to refer to Euratom's provisions directly – not through §2 para. (1) of Atomic Law.

The literature on the subject points to the uniqueness of the regulatory framework of the Constitution when it comes to regulating the matter of radioactive waste.[42] The constitutional legislator did not end at establishing a general entitlement to generate electricity using nuclear fuel.[43] The adopted method involved regulating the issue of radioactive waste by isolating it from the overall domain of nuclear energy.[44] This emphasised the significance of this subject matter.[45] It was taken into consideration already in the 1959 amendment to the Constitution. The amounts of radioactive waste existing at the time must have been marginal. But this did not prevent the decision-makers from incorporating an appropriate regulation into the Constitution. This proves the high quality of the amendment because it regulated the matter of nuclear energy holistically and extensively.

The notion of "the disposal of radioactive substances" from Article 74 (1) item 11a of the German Constitution encompasses several subject matters with its range of meaning. The most important one pertains to the processing of radioactive waste.[46] The sole act of "disposal of radioactive waste" encompasses also the disposal of radioactive materials generated in the process of production of energy from these materials.[47] This concerns also radioactive materials produced in relation to the utilisation of nuclear energy for other purposes than energy production.[48] An example are radioactive substances generated as a result of the application of ionising radiation in medicine. The constitutional notion of "the disposal of radioactive waste" covers also the subject matter of radioactive contamination of airspace, water or other features of our environment.[49]

Article 73(1) item 14 of the Constitution grants the lawmaker the right to choose the manner of disposal of waste (i.e. if this waste is to be stored right away or if the radioactive waste that may be recycled, such as spent fuel fit for reprocessing, should be reprocessed).[50]

Article 73(1) item 14 of *Grundgesetz* addresses also the issue of storage of radioactive waste. This concerns both interim storage as well as disposal (i.e. in fact permanent storage) of radioactive waste.[51] Interim storage of radioactive waste involves temporarily isolating such waste from an environment inhabited by humans – in broader terms, from the biosphere – until this waste is managed further. Permanent storage of radioactive waste, in turn, makes use of a method of final management of radioactive waste, which involves creating such conditions for the permanent storage of this waste that prevent the radiation generated by this waste as a result of its partial decay with the natural passing of time (i.e. its half-life) from exceeding the adopted limits. Since in the case of some radioactive elements, the time required for the radiation they generate to drop as a result of their natural decay to a level that does not pose a threat to human health and life is over one million years, the term "permanent storage" is referred to as "disposal".[52]

Moreover, the German constitutional regulation also encompasses issues related to the construction of facilities designed for the disposal, management and utilisation of radioactive waste.[53] The said constitutional provision also addresses the issue of the location of industrial establishments processing radioactive waste.[54]

The views of law doctrine, as well as the established line of judicial decisions point to the need for a broader interpretation of the competence of the Federation in the area of the disposal of radioactive substances.[55] This arises from the need to cover the future, new methods of disposal of radioactive waste by this competence.[56] It is reasonable to accept such a manner of understanding of the provisions of *Grundgesetz*. One needs a dynamic interpretation of the competence-related provision in question. This is due to the protective nature of this provision – the Federation should not be deprived of a way to act in the domain of the disposal of radioactive waste if new methods of disposal of radioactive waste become available.

A more in-depth analysis of Germany's Constitution in this context makes it possible for the content of Article 73(1) item 14 of the Constitution to encompass also methods of "true" disposal of radioactive waste.[57] It is a highly valuable observation. Referring to "true" methods of radioactive waste disposal defines the present state of scientific knowledge and the technological progress made in this area. It also encompasses the criticism of the current state of affairs, which involves developing methods of utilisation of nuclear energy to produce electricity at an industrial scale. This takes place, however, without making use of the available technologies of disposal of radioactive waste. This criticism is legitimate for two reasons. First, it was expressed in the past tense – the methods currently in use have nothing to do with the disposal of radioactive waste. They involve merely physically separating sources of radioactive radiation from the environment where humans are or may be present. The essence of the methods applied today is long-term protection of the biosphere by physically isolating humans from sources of radioactive radiation.[58] At the same time, the established limitations are to prevent the migration of radioactive waste to the natural environment.[59] The idea is in particular to prevent the spread of radioactive elements across the soil and the penetration of such elements into groundwater or surface water.[60] The contemporary methods of radioactive waste management do not eliminate the very source of radioactive radiation. They involve waiting for the radioactive radiation level to drop as a result of the natural cycle of isotope decay. The period of permanent storage could end with the drop of the level or radioactive radiation below the permissible limits. Every radioactive element has a different half-life. In the case of uranium 235, it is a period of nearly 700 million years. In the case of plutonium, it is about 87 years. This means that uranium 235 contained in radioactive waste will reach a radiation level below the permitted limits as a result of its natural decay after a much longer period of time than the planned minimum lifespan of the dedicated radioactive waste disposal site.[61] The current standard policy is to store radioactive waste at installations (interim storage or disposal sites) isolated from humans and the natural environment until the said period of time passes.[62] The most important aspect here is to make sure that these nuclear installations are able to operate safely for a long time, expressed in millennia.[63] This is because within 2–3 generations such a waste was generated that will burden ca. 40,000 future generations.[64]

On account of the very long period of decay of plutonium or uranium, the contemporary methods do not actually "truly" dispose of radioactive radiation. Another idea underlying the said methods is that the future will bring technologies enabling neutralisation of radioactive waste (above the undesired levels). An example of a technology that may involve "true" disposal of radioactive waste is the de-radiation of radioactive waste (*Entstrahlung*).[65] It involves accelerating the natural period of decay of radioactive isotopes through transmutation.[66] Another – less ground-breaking – solution may be deepening of processing of spent fuel involving separating (decomposing) such radioactive material and retrieving an even greater amount of elements from it.[67] This way, the radioactivity of final waste would be reduced.[68] Therefore, the period of storing radioactive waste physically separated from the natural environment would become considerably shorter.

In the 1970s, the period of adoption of the first statutory measure aimed at neutralising radioactive waste, the idea must have been based on an expected scientific and technological breakthrough in the domain of radioactive waste disposal. Meanwhile, interim storage of spent fuel was supposed to make it possible to last out safely until the state of knowledge is sufficient to neutralise spent fuel effectively. This interpretation of the statutory regulations of the time was supported also by a concept promoted in the late 1980s, according to which radioactive waste should be stored temporarily (on the surface of the earth) for 30 to 100 years. This "waiting" period should be then used to devise an optimal way to dispose of radioactive waste.[69] But a completely different interpretation of the original statutory concept is possible as well. It could involve postponing the problem to make it something to deal with by future generations, regardless of whether any suitable technological measures are available. The interpretation of the lawmaker's original intentions does not have to be correct, though. But the fact that there is no big difference between the solution involving organising interim storage sites, kept "alive" for dozens of years with a hope for a technological breakthrough and the concept of leaving the problem for future generations to handle sounds like a paradox. The conclusion that can be drawn is that it was a cynical and calculated strategy of putting the problem off for the future.

Such an approach seems to be typical of the French nuclear energy sector:

> Intermediate- and high-level long-lived waste which we produce at present is the final waste of our generation; it is currently impossible to reprocess it for both safety and economic reasons. In the future, it will surely be possible to reduce the radiotoxicity of waste.[70]

This concept is based on a belief that the coming technological advancement will make it possible to solve the problem of waste. But this advancement may be limited only to the processing of new waste, and the technological solutions available may be not suitable to handle the radioactive waste already processed – e.g. vitrified. The above idea is accompanied by a conviction that the issue may be left unsolved to future generations.

Meanwhile, the approach of the German public opinion and the German lawmaker is totally different. Moreover, the German concept of final disposal of radioactive waste currently in place involves a departure from the earlier approach, which involved leaving the problem of disposal of radioactive waste to future generations to handle. The rationale for the federal act *Standortasuwahlgesetz* states clearly that its purpose is to address and solve the problem in the lifetime of the current generation.[71]

This is why one of the probable scenarios involves establishing a permanent site for the disposal of radioactive waste, designed in a way that prevents this waste from being recovered to the surface later on[72] (e.g. when solutions enabling the de-radiation of radioactive waste are already available). Regardless of whether waste is stored with the prospect of natural decay of isotopes or with a hope for the necessary technological developments to come, the problem of radioactive waste management is being postponed. One should therefore acknowledge that both the past and the present methods of disposal of radioactive waste do not involve "true" disposal.

At the same time, the German Federal Constitutional Court has already addressed the question about the constitutionality of a concept of neutralisation of radioactive waste which is not a "true" method of disposal of radioactive waste.[73] A relevant case, ref. no. 1 BvR 2456/06, was decided in 2008. The complainant argued to prove the non-compliance of a solution based on a system of interim radioactive waste storage sites established on the premises of nuclear power plants with Article 2 (2) sentence 1 of the German Constitution.[74] The main reason for the claimed unconstitutionality was to be the lack of an ultimate concept of disposal of radioactive waste. Another reason was the fact that no technical measures of disposal of radioactive waste were (and still are) provided.[75] But the FCC addressed and interpreted the claim quite differently. The Court found that the claim pointed to a question of whether it was constitutionally acceptable to use nuclear energy to commercially generate electricity in the light of no solutions enabling permanent storage of radioactive waste being adopted.[76] According to the FCC, the fact that the nuclear reactors were supposed to be shut down by 2022 did not affect the said circumstances.[77] The Court stated that it was not obliged to answer the question asked, although it actually reformulated it itself. It was not stated directly by the FCC, but the existing body of judicial decisions might suggest that the answer should be given by the legislative authority, which stems from a reference to the judgement issued in the Kalkar case.[78] The Court found then that the 1959 amendment to the Constitution, involving an addition of new constitutional competence provided to the federal lawmaker, involved acceptability of the use of nuclear energy to commercially generate electricity.[79] The ultimate decision of whether to use nuclear energy or not rests exclusively with the federal lawmaker.[80] According to the Court, the above was confirmed by the 2006 reform of the federal system, the so-called *Föderalismusreform*. The constitutional lawmaker did not implement then any changes regarding the actual scope of authority of the federal lawmaker in the area in question. The only change was the transfer of the legislation in the domain of nuclear energy (including the disposal of radioactive substances) to the list of exclusive powers of the federal lawmaker while maintaining the essence of the power in question.[81] Nevertheless, one should notice that the Court made a significant simplification by limiting the question about the final concept of disposal of radioactive waste being production-ready only to the matter of acceptability of the use of nuclear energy. This meant making do with the Court's own existing standpoint on nuclear energy. The Court did not, in fact, solve the matter of constitutional acceptability of common use of makeshift solutions in the form of interim storage sites.

The German Constitution offers one morc competence-related ground to the federal lawmaker in connection with the issue of radioactive waste. Article 73 (1) item 14 of Germany's Constitution reads as follows:

> Art. 73. 1. The Federation shall have exclusive legislative power with respect to: . . .
>
> 14) . . . protection against hazards arising from the release of nuclear energy or from ionising radiation, and the disposal of radioactive substances.

The regulation encompasses the protection against hazards related to radioactive waste.[82] This includes also radiation used for medical purposes.[83] Some authors understand the scope of the said provisions even broader and claim that it covers also the protection against hazards originating from domains like engineering, science, industry, business, agriculture, or education.[84] Interpreting the said provisions in such broad terms is wrong because they were introduced in 1959, in a reality completely different from today's. Also, extending the scope of the Constitution to include the said provisions was connected with the initiation of commercial use of nuclear energy. The Federation was granted power also in this area, which is why the scope of this power should be applied in relation to radiation originating from the usage of nuclear energy.

Article 73(1) item 14 of *Grundgesetz* regulates also the issue of elimination of hazards "arising from the release of nuclear energy or from ionising radiation, and the disposal of radioactive substances", which have already occurred.[85] Such an understanding and interpretation of the content of the Constitution points to several possible scenarios. First, it concerns situations of release of nuclear energy within the territory of the Federal Republic of Germany.[86] Second, it will also include releases of nuclear energy beyond the borders of the Federal Republic of Germany.[87] Third, the provision will also encompass radioactive radiation occurring within the area of the Federal Republic of Germany.[88] Fourth, it will also concern radioactive radiation occurring outside the Federal Republic of Germany.[89] This means that the scope of protection against hazards covers all possible scenarios of impact of nuclear energy within the territory under the jurisdiction of German state authorities.

In the event of release of radioactive radiation from a nuclear power plant, the legal grounds of Article 73(1) item 14 of *Grundgesetz* covers all causes of such an event. First, it will be internal causes, like a failure of a nuclear power plant.[90] Second, the content of Article 73(1) item 14 of the Constitution covers also natural but external causes (e.g. earthquakes). Third, the content of said article pertains also to radioactive radiation caused by man (e.g. as a result of a terrorist attack on a nuclear reactor or some other nuclear installation).[91] Fourth, the provisions in question will also cover the effects of application of nuclear energy for military purposes.[92] The considered article will therefore act as the legal grounds to act in matters involving the occurrence of radiation as a result of warfare.

The entire regulation under Article 73(1) item 14 of Grundgesetz regarding the "disposal of radioactive waste" and the "protection against hazards arising from the release of nuclear energy or from ionising radiation, and the disposal of radioactive substances" concerns only the peaceful application of nuclear energy. But the "protection against hazards arising from the release of nuclear energy or from ionising radiation, and the disposal of radioactive substances" involves protection against the effects of both peaceful and non-peaceful utilisation of nuclear energy.[93] From the point of view of legislative power, it does (and should) not matter if the existing radioactive radiation originates from the peaceful utilisation of nuclear energy or not. It may be an outcome of hostile, non-peaceful, or military application of nuclear energy.[94] In the end, the effect is going to be the same as that triggered by a source involving the peaceful application of nuclear energy as the hazard posed to humans or the potential contamination will entail the same consequences. Such an interpretation of the content of Article 73 (1) item 14 of the Constitution as to the protection against radioactive radiation will therefore include the effects of both military action and acts of terrorism. An example will include the use of so-called dirty bombs,[95] also known as "improvised nuclear weapons".[96] This involves using explosives combined with radioactive substances. Such a device might feature not only "pure" plutonium but also radioactive waste. A "dirty bomb" may also contain dangerous chemicals.[97] Detonation of an "improvised nuclear weapon" would cause the radioactive substances contained inside to spread over a large area, which would then lead to immediate contamination. Using a "professional" (military) nuclear weapon, obtained as a result of e.g. theft, would be even more dangerous. Another scenario might involve a direct attack on a nuclear reactor or other nuclear installations.[98] Attacks on radioactive waste storage sites[99] and on installations which process and concentrate spent fuel would be therefore especially threatening. This is, of course, because there are great amounts of radioactive substances stored at such facilities. Depending on the installation type, these might be even only the most hazardous – radioactive – waste, i.e. high-level radioactive waste. All these situations are covered by the scope of application of the provisions of Article 73 (1) item 14 of the German Constitution.

Article 73(1) item 14 of *Grundgesetz* grants the Federation the legislative power to provide "protection against hazards arising from the release of nuclear energy or from ionising radiation, and the disposal of radioactive substances". The notion of "hazards" covers its interpretation based on the statutory regulations as well as preventive measures and actions.[100] It is also argued in this context that one should not limit oneself to preventive measures understood in technical terms only.[101] The actions undertaken should consider different scenarios, expectations and forecasts regarding the possible scenarios of events.[102] The protection against hazards, referred to in Article 73 (1) item 14 of the Constitution, involves therefore preventing such hazards, curbing the development of such hazards, eliminating these hazards and rectifying the damage that has already occurred.[103] Such a broad interpretation of this provision, encompassing also protection and preventive measures, stems from the protective purpose of Article 73(1) item 14 of *Grundgesetz*.[104]

On account of the different sources of radiation, the applicable regulation has been shaped by the legislator as broadly as possible.[105] The legislative power of the Federation will therefore also include protection against hazards resulting from the processing of spent fuel.[106] Moreover, it includes also protection against hazards related to the transportation of radioactive waste.[107] One should notice here that unlike in the case of the standard regulation on waste, the transportation of radioactive waste is subject to separate regulations.[108] The content of Article 73(1) item 14 of the German Constitution is also the basis for regulations governing the protection against radiation originating from the storage of radioactive waste.[109]

The legislator has enforced Article 73(1) item 14 of the Constitution in relation to radioactive waste by amending Atomic Law and incorporating a new regulatory framework included in the new provision §9a on radioactive waste. This legislative power served as the basis to adopt *Standortauswahlgesetz*.[110]

To recapitulate, one should acknowledge that the provisions of Article 73(1) item 14 of *Grundgesetz*, which address the subject matter of radioactive waste, encompass not only neutralising radioactive waste but also preventing hazards originating from radioactive radiation. Sources of such radiation – apart from radioactive waste – may also include any other sources of radioactive radiation. As a result, the potential area of impact of the German Constitution in this domain is quite extensive.

3. Regulatory approach to radioactive waste in Atomic Law

The constitutional regulation expressed in Article 73(1) item 14 of *Grundgesetz* in relation to the "radioactive waste disposal" had not found expression in statutory solutions for a long time. The legislator's and lawmaker's decisions on the utilisation of nuclear energy were not accompanied by a statutory regulation addressing the manner of dealing with radioactive waste. Apart from the already discussed constitutional regulation on the disposal of radioactive substances, no statutory regulation was proposed in 1959 to accompany it.[111]

It was only 1974 when the Federal Government offered a concept of disposal of radioactive waste.[112] It was based on a plan of establishment of a centralised installation designed to neutralise radioactive waste (*Entsorgungspark*) imported from the entire Federation.[113] It was supposed to be the world's largest spent fuel reprocessing installation.[114] As for the very term of "Entsorgungspark", used by people from the nuclear sector, given its euphemistic nature, it was compared to expressions typical of the national-socialist propaganda.[115] The said centralised installation was supposed to be used to: store radioactive waste, process spent fuel and produce fuel rods in the place of the final (permanent) spent fuel storage facility.[116] The potential location considered was Gorleben in Lower Saxony.[117] According to item 6 of the decision of representatives of the Federal Government and of the Länder of 28 September 1979, the research operations to be carried out in Gorleben were to be started immediately.[118] They were to provide the necessary knowledge about the deposits of rock salt (halite) in Gorleben, which would make it possible to consider and proceed with appropriate projects in the second half of 1980s.[119] At the same time, the final disposal site was to be set up by 2000.[120] In order to make sure that the new centralised installation is able to operate at full capacity, in 1975 the Federal Government adopted a requirement according to which it was necessary to determine the method of management of all radioactive waste to be produced at the nuclear installation intended to be built in the request for permission to build a new nuclear power plant.[121]

On account of the above, it was only in 1976, the year of adoption of the so-called 4th Amendment to Atomic Law, when the first statutory regulation dealing with radioactive waste appeared.[122] The incorporation of regulations dealing with radioactive waste into Atomic Law was motivated also by purely practical reasons. Since the mid-1960s, the existing radioactive waste storage sites were in danger of becoming overfilled.[123] Also, the nuclear industry and the operational launch of subsequent nuclear installations called for a need to regulate the matter of radioactive waste.[124]

Paradoxically, the lack of regulations posed a greater regulatory risk for energy enterprises because the possible outcome of adoption of new regulations was difficult to predict.

The quoted amendment to Atomic Law could have been viewed as a solution which made the "polluter pays" principle actually practised and respected. In this case, the costs would have to be borne by the producers of radioactive waste. The operators of nuclear reactors have had the greatest share in the production of all the radioactive waste that needs to be currently managed.[125] The "polluter pays" principle obliged those who produce pollution (radioactive waste) to dispose of it or bear the costs of such disposal. It is argued, however, that its original purpose was to organise the input for the reprocessing installation planned to be built in Gorleben.[126]

The statutory regulations dealing with radioactive waste have changed and evolved over time. Today, the entire statutory regulation addressing the issue of radioactive waste is contained in §9a of Atomic Law. It regulates the manner of managing spent fuel, irradiated parts of dismantled nuclear installations or other radioactive substances of different origin. At first, there were two ways to dispose of radioactive waste: "non-detrimental utilisation" (statutory term: *schadlose Verwertung*) and direct disposal (statutory term: *direkte Endlagerung*).[127] This division stemmed directly from Atomic Law. It is quite confusing, though. First, the site for the permanent storage (disposal) of high-level radioactive waste has not been created yet (or anywhere in the world).[128] Second, the content of the act may have suggested that "non-detrimental utilisation" of radioactive waste is fully safe and does not lead to the generation of radioactive waste in the process. But it is quite different, actually. The "non-detrimental utilisation" of waste in the process of the production of nuclear fuel leads to the generation of almost exclusively high-level radioactive waste as a by-product.[129]

The division based on Atomic Law, proposing the notions of "non-detrimental utilisation" and "direct disposal", corresponds also with the French division into the "open fuel cycle" and the "closed fuel cycle".[130] But it is similarly imprecise in terms of the notions adopted and used. A closed fuel cycle is one which does not generate significant amounts of high-level radioactive waste in the process of fuel production. Nowadays, it is possible to retrieve virtually the entire amount of non-used uranium and plutonium from spent fuel.[131] It does not mean, however, that the fuel cycle is closed when the process generates non-recyclable high-level radioactive waste.

A much more accurate division is one into indirect disposal of radioactive waste with prior reprocessing of spent fuel (*indirekte Endlagerung mit Wiederaufarbeitung*) and direct disposal without prior reprocessing of spent fuel (*direkte Endlagerung ohne Wiederaufarbeitung*).[132]

The former was to involve a "non-detrimental recovery" of radioactive waste. The idea was to reprocess used radioactive material. The latter is about first qualifying a given radioactive material as radioactive waste, and then, after it is sorted accordingly, neutralising it. Regardless of whether a given type of waste is classified into the former or the latter category, it will be eventually neutralised through direct (final) disposal (*direkte Endlagerung*). The official definition of the process in question is provided in §9a para. (1) sentence 1 of Atomic Law.

4. The problem of reprocessing of spent fuel

In the initial period of the new provisions of Atomic Law on radioactive waste being in force, the standard practice involved reprocessing any used radioactive material first.[133] Only when the existing technical solutions did not make it economically feasible to reprocess radioactive material, or if such reprocessing was contrary to the purposes defined in Article 1(1) items 2–4 of Atomic Law, was it acceptable to transfer radioactive waste directly to a dedicated storage facility.[134] It was in line with the 1974 concept of disposal of radioactive waste. The precedence of reprocessing was motivated by the intention to reintroduce unused sources of energy obtained from spent fuel (especially uranium 235 and plutonium 239) into the national economy.[135] Only two methods of disposal of waste were available at the time, both defined in Atomic Law.[136] The other method (direct disposal) concerned radioactive waste that was not suitable for reprocessing.[137] It was only with the adoption of the Act of 19 July 1994, amending the Atomic Law,[138] when the statutory precedence of reprocessing of spent fuel was abolished.[139]

If a nuclear power plant operator decided to reprocess nuclear fuel, they had to prove, in line with Article 9a(1a) of Atomic Law, that they were able to guarantee that the recovered plutonium would be used only in installations earmarked for commercial production of electric energy. Article 9a(1a) offered a possibility to utilise recovered plutonium in domestic or foreign installations. In the case of domestic installations (operating within the framework of Atomic Law) it was obligatory to prove that there was a demand for a specific amount of plutonium. As for foreign installations, it was necessary to provide an official certificate of transfer of rights to use given fissile materials in order to utilise them in a foreign commercial installation.

This method of management of spent fuel was practised until the adoption of *Atomausstieg I*. This radioactive waste management was based on a concept recognising the need for the reprocessing of spent fuel. The concept was highly popular in the late 1970s and early 1980s in particular. The assumption made on its basis then was that it would soon be possible to arrive at a closed nuclear fuel cycle.[140] The very method of spent fuel reprocessing was about recovering uranium and plutonium from spent fuel.[141] It involved applying a process of thermal recycling.[142] It was a form of disposal of the generated radioactive waste[143] and was supposed to satisfy the demands formulated on the grounds of the adopted environmental protection policy.[144] The process of reprocessing spent fuel was to make the process of utilisation of this fuel almost 50% effective.[145] Another reason for the application of the process in question was the fact that it made it possible to produce much more electric energy using plutonium than using uranium in the same amount.[146] At the same time, plutonium is unique in that it regenerates itself,[147] which could have been a chance to arrive at a closed fuel cycle with the necessary technological developments becoming reality.

Apart from the need for technological progress, which would make it possible to reduce the amount of radioactive waste produced, there was also an argument for a "moral duty" in this regard.[148] The nuclear energy sector would use the argument of "moral duty" most likely because the said process was not profitable.[149] In the 1980s, when the method of reprocessing of spent fuel was still used in practice, it was estimated that the reprocessing of spent fuel was almost 50% more expensive than the method of underground storage of spent fuel.[150] But the publicly given reason behind proceeding with this unprofitable activity was a social reason – protection of the natural environment.[151] Other reasons which were to justify the necessity to invest in this activity included energy security, reducing the volume of radioactive waste, creating jobs, and implementing the country's policy through the development of new technologies.[152] It seems that the nuclear energy sector's talk of a "moral duty" did not have anything to do with the "polluter pays" principle, but was actually motivated by a necessity to manage the generated radioactive waste. It could also justify the unprofitability of the adopted process. Extending the nuclear fuel cycle led to the development of the nuclear energy sector as a branch of economy as the situation led to the establishment of completely new nuclear installations, designed to e.g. reprocess spent fuel.

The reuse of uranium, fossil fuel, saved natural resources.[153] As the Federal Republic of Germany imported uranium, it was dependent on its suppliers.[154] The German Democratic Republic had its own uranium mine at the time. It was argued that the import of both resources and technology (e.g. used to enrich uranium) was limited by states which had access to them, even the democratic ones.[155] The process of recovery of nuclear fuel aimed at improving the state's energy security by making the state less dependent on the import of uranium as fossil fuel.[156] It was even considered in the German government's energy policy in the 1970s as a way to make the state independent from the import of energy resources.[157] Moreover, importing resources involves a foreign exchange risk (risk of differences in the currency exchange rates). As a result, the final cost of fuel depends not only on the fluctuation of prices of the imported goods (uranium or plutonium) but also on the currency exchange rate at the moment of purchase or based on the exchange rate according to the concluded long-term contract for the supply of a given resource.[158]

Supporters of the reprocessing of spent fuel argued also with the threat of near depletion of uranium resources.[159] This pertains especially to countries which have a significant number of commercial reactors. If they obtained fuel only for some of those reactors by utilising the technology of reprocessing of spent fuel, it would minimise the threat of uncertainty of supplies.[160] All this provided an even stronger stimulus to work on a technology enabling the recovery of nuclear fuel.[161] But not many countries could actually invest in this solution because the biggest obstacle to making practical use of it is having a significant number of nuclear reactors. This is because one needs considerable amounts of spent fuel from high-capacity industrial reactors to achieve the necessary returns to scale.[162]

There are many arguments against the reprocessing of radioactive waste. The most important of them is that the plan to organise a closed fuel cycle has not been carried out since it was first presented 40 years ago.[163] Using plutonium to produce electric energy generates much more radioactive waste.[164] But thanks to the reprocessing of spent fuel, it is possible to reduce the mass of spent fuel by almost 90%.[165] This is why it is not so uncommon to come across opinions according to which it is better to have smaller amounts of high-level radioactive waste than huge amounts of radioactive waste originating directly from spent fuel.[166]

Moreover, the international community has undertaken many initiatives aimed to stop the spread of nuclear weapons (non-proliferation of nuclear weapons).[167] Meanwhile, processing spent fuel may foil these efforts[168] because the process involves utilising greater amounts of plutonium.[169] According to the opinions against the processing of spent fuel, the process expands the group of entities having access to nuclear weapons,[170] or at least to plutonium. One needs 10 kg of plutonium to make an atomic bomb,[171] but it is enough to have a fraction of this amount to make a dirty bomb. Germany has already had cases of illegal trading of plutonium, or cases of utilisation of plutonium in installations other than supervised nuclear installations.[172] One of the solutions considered was to implement an international mechanism of plutonium storage,[173] but the idea was abandoned. Another proposed method to deal with the problem involved creating a global network of installations designed to recover plutonium by reprocessing spent fuel.[174] The activity of these installations was to be subject to mutual inspections carried out by the parties (states) involved in the project.[175] In the 1980s, the reprocessing of spent fuel was booming. It was argued then to implement the limitations under the adopted policy of non-proliferation of nuclear weapons not by creating significant risks to security or by imposing excessive financial burdens. Those in favour of further reprocessing of spent fuel believed that the said solutions were excessive safety measures.[176] After nearly 40 years, considering the present level of terrorist threat, it is impossible to uphold the argument for the relaxation of the adopted safety measures and for the minimisation of the expenses involved in the former. Moreover, the installations designed to reprocess radioactive substances – especially plutonium – may act as the perfect disguise for military operations.[177] This means enriching radioactive substances and obtaining parameters suitable for military purposes. Germany's efforts aimed at developing nuclear technologies in the 1960s gave rise to concerns that those initiatives were undertaken with military purposes in mind. Those concerns were dispelled with the adoption of an international framework of maintenance of installations used to process spent fuel by Germany, Great Britain and the Netherlands.[178] But the composition of the isotopes found in the plutonium recovered in the course of the reprocessing of spent fuel makes it impossible to utilise it for military purposes.[179] It is true in the case of reprocessed plutonium in relation to some installations. But some other installations may make it possible to utilise the element for military purposes.[180] It is also possible to use plutonium to make dirty bombs. All this makes it highly difficult to make sure that plutonium itself[181] and the high-level radioactive waste it generates are physically secure.

In the years 1971–1991, Germany operated a nuclear research installation in Karlsruhe (*Versuchs-Wiederaufarbeitungsanlage Karlsruhe*),[182] designed to reprocess spent fuel. The costs of constructing and running the installation were borne by the Federal Government.[183] Its capacity was approximately 200 tonnes of nuclear fuel per year.[184] But it was too little compared to the increase in the amount of spent fuel at the time. Therefore, in 1977, 12 energy companies established a special purpose vehicle named *Deutsche Gesselschaft für Wiederaufarbeitung von Kernbrennstoffen (DWK)*, which was to build a nuclear spent fuel reprocessing installation – offering greater, commercial-level capacities.[185] The original plan was to locate it in Gorleben on account of the concept of the establishment of a centralised facility for disposal of nuclear waste.[186] There were long-lasting mass protests against the launch of the installation in question.[187] In 1979 a decision was made to change the 1974 concept, which involved centralised disposal of radioactive waste in Gorleben.[188] Based on the new integrated concept of disposal of such waste (*integriertes Entsorgungskonzept*), a decision was made to process spent fuel abroad until a suitable nuclear installation is set up in Germany.[189] In 1985, after the idea to locate the installation in Gorleben was abandoned, DWK proceeded with the construction works in Bavarian Wackersdorf (*Wiederaufarbeitungsanlage Wackersdorf*).[190] The capacity of the new nuclear installation, set to be put into operation in 1996, was to range from 350 to 500 tonnes per year, depending on the demand.[191] But the project was suspended in 1989.[192] The intention to build a nuclear installation in Wackersdorf was eventually abandoned.[193] In the meantime, there were long-term contracts regarding the reprocessing of spent fuel from German reactors in French and British nuclear installations concluded on the grounds of private law.[194] These private law contracts were supported in 1991 by international agreements concluded by Germany and France and by Germany and England.[195] They included an obligation according to which the supplies of spent fuel from German power plants could not be subject to any legal or administrative restrictions.[196]

In order to deal with high-level radioactive waste remaining after the nuclear installation in Karlsruhe, an installation designed to vitrify this waste was built nearby.[197] A permit to operate this installation for 18 months was granted in 2009.[198] After the set time, sufficient to vitrify all of the remaining waste, the installation was shut down and decontaminated.

According to the literature on the subject, the process of reprocessing of spent fuel is also subject to certain constitutional requirements.[199] In the light of the above view, the constitutional standards stipulate that safety is more important than supporting the development of the nuclear energy sector, which means that safety is also more important than the reprocessing of spent fuel.[200] When considering arguments speaking in favour of or against the reprocessing of spent fuel, one should focus in particular on the security of the installations involved in the process. Only if such installations are officially recognised as safe can one consider the matter of reprocessing spent fuel further.

5. Transportation of spent fuel

In 1991, the Karlsruhe spent fuel reprocessing installation was shut down.[201] At the same time, it was decided to abandon the initiated construction of the spent fuel reprocessing installation in Wackersdorf.[202] From then on, it was possible to reprocess used fuel rods by recovering radioactive substances only abroad.[203] At the same time, the political and legal conflict connected with the reprocessing of spent fuel grew stronger.[204] The legal concerns focused mainly on the security of this method (*schadlose Verwertung*) within the meaning of §9a para. (1) of Atomic Law.[205] The main claim in this context was to have the reprocessing of spent fuel taking place abroad correspond to German safety standards.[206] Meanwhile, foreign nuclear installations did not meet the German requirements concerning state guarantees for the safety and protection of public health.[207] Also, the fact that there was no nuclear installation used to reprocess spent fuel in Germany gave rise to a question about the possibility to maintain the validity of permits already given to German nuclear power plants.[208] After a possible closure of access to foreign nuclear installations designed to reprocess spent fuel, German nuclear reactors would not have managed to fulfill the obligation to reprocess the existing spent fuel, which was still binding.[209] The views of legal academics and commentators, as well as the established line of judicial decisions saw attempts to argue for acceptability of the reprocessing of spent fuel from German power plants in foreign nuclear installations.[210] The above legal doubts were eventually dispelled in 1994 with the amendment of Atomic Law, which provided for abolishing the possibility to manage spent fuel by means of spent fuel reprocessing.[211]

Further major changes were brought about by the so-called *Atomausstieg I.* The provisions of part IV item 2 of the agreement of 14 June 2000 concluded between the Federal Government of Germany and the country's energy enterprises regarding the reprocessing of spent fuel stipulated that the disposal of radioactive waste from nuclear power plants would be limited from 1 July 2005 onwards only to direct (final) disposal.[212] Until the said date it was still permitted to transport spent fuel for reprocessing purposes, and any spent fuel supplied before 1 July 2005 but not accepted by could still be processed.[213] The political arrangements included in the said agreement were expressed in the following legal regulations. The act of 22 April 2002, amending Atomic Law, imposed a ban on exportation of used radioactive material outside the country from 1 July 2005 onwards.[214] According to §9a para. (1) sentence 2 of Atomic Law, it was forbidden to deliver irradiated nuclear fuel originating from the operation of installations for the fission of nuclear fuel for the commercial generation of electricity to an installation for the reprocessing of irradiated nuclear fuel for the purposes of non-detrimental utilisation as of 1 July 2005. There was a question about whether the lawmaker could actually ban the processing of spent fuel abroad as of 2005 at all.[215] Another important aspect was also to determine whether the lawmaker should bear liability for damages towards the said energy companies.[216] The intention to impose the ban only in 2005 had to do with the contracts and agreements being in force at the time as they were valid until 2005 (with a possible extension up to 2015).[217] At the same time, the content of §9a para. (1) made it possible to extend this date in exceptional situations. The set statutory date of imposition of the ban (with an option of extension), which corresponded to the expiry date of the contracts and agreements on the reprocessing of spent fuel, postponed the liability for damages. Also, it did not violate the terms of the international agreements concluded with France and England since their purpose was to reinforce the validity of the contracts and agreements concluded on the grounds of private law and the date set by the German lawmaker did not interfere in any way with the essentials thereof. The scope of the lawmaker's interference concerned only the lack of possibility to extend the date of validity of those contracts and agreements. Postponing the imposition of the ban for a few years was motivated by problems with the capacity of the existing interim radioactive waste storage sites.[218] In order to prevent the storage sites from becoming overfilled, the Federal Government decided to extend the period of allowed transfer of spent fuel to foreign nuclear installations.[219]

In the rationale for the amendments to Atomic Law, arising from the political arrangements made in relation to *Atomausstieg I*, one can see an intention to prevent the spread (proliferation) of nuclear weapons and to limit the potential threats caused by the transportation of radioactive substances.[220] Therefore, one of the two ways of dealing with radioactive waste became impracticable because the reprocessing of spent fuel was banned as of 2005.[221] The said new regulation was one of the key elements of the first nuclear phaseout (*Atomausstieg I*). The implemented limitations were an aftermath of huge social protests on the routes on which radioactive waste had been transported since the 1970s.[222] The social conflicts of the time escalated so much that the situation tended to be compared to a civil war.[223] But it was, in fact, a form of objection to the use of nuclear energy. There were attempts to stop trains transporting radioactive waste which was a by-product of spent fuel processing. There were even cases of destruction of railway infrastructure.[224] Some groups aimed to make the costs of guarding and protecting the rolling stock so high that it would become unreasonable and unjustified to spend public funds to cover them.[225] The expected consequence of incurring such significant costs was to be a withdrawal of the existing political support, which was to lead to a halt in the transportation of radioactive substances. Such a course of events would have been a factor that would have considerably limited any further development of the nuclear energy sector in Germany.

Looking back on the situation years later, one can say that both the peaceful initiatives and the practical forms of civil disobedience that shaped the reality of the time resulted in the expected political outcomes. Another direct consequence of the adoption of *Atomausstieg I* for the matter of abandonment of the production of electric energy in nuclear reactors will be a curb on the increase in the amount of the radioactive waste produced (in commercial nuclear reactors) by 2022.[226] But this does not mean that the amount of the generated radioactive waste will start dropping because the domain of radioactive waste management is governed by different rules than, for instance, the domain of municipal waste management, where a part of this waste is subject to natural decay. From the perspective of the transportation of radioactive waste, *Atomausstieg I* opened a way to end the transportation of radioactive waste. Soon after the adoption of *Atomausstieg I* it was argued that defining an end date for the transportation of radioactive waste was (paradoxically) the only opportunity to foster an atmosphere of social approval for the transportation itself and to make sure that the process of transportation runs without interruptions.[227]

Another reason for the mass social protests were concerns for safety. Spent fuel was transported to spent fuel processing installations in northern France (La Hague) or in Great Britain (Sellafield). The scale of the transportation operations can be described best using the relevant data from 2000. There were over 4,000 tonnes of high-level radioactive waste to be collected from both of those installations.[228] It was necessary to organise over 400 shipments.[229] Recovering radioactive waste meant more frequent transportation of nuclear fuel itself (import of nuclear fuel, export of spent fuel, import of regenerated nuclear fuel, transportation of remaining radioactive waste) than in the case of a one-off use of fuel rods (import of nuclear fuel and export of spent fuel to an interim storage or disposal facility). It is estimated that the number of shipments of radioactive materials dropped by approximately a third.[230] It was therefore also a form of fulfilment of the obligation to minimise the exposure of humans and the natural environment to radioactive radiation, as required under §6 of the federal Radiation Protection Ordinance (*Strahlenschutzverordnung*) of 20 July 2001.[231]

The 2005 ban on the transportation of spent fuel to installations processing such material in France and Great Britain has been analysed also from the perspective of its compliance with the law of the European Union.[232] Euratom established a common nuclear market, which includes services such as the processing of spent fuel.[233] The ban on exporting spent fuel abroad was therefore a measure violating the freedom to provide services (free movement of services).[234] Such a measure would be justifiable in the area of limitation of the transportation of radioactive material provided that all of the radioactive material is placed ultimately in a radioactive waste disposal facility.[235] As for the extent to which the said limitation is to contribute to the protection of the natural environment, it is stressed that such a limitation implemented under the German legislation could be justified if it applied to installations located in Germany.[236] Meanwhile, it pertains, in fact, to nuclear installations processing spent fuel, which are located elsewhere, in the territories of other Member States. The German regulation is therefore not relevant in this context.[237] But it needs to be noted that the reduction of the volume of spent fuel translates, for instance, to a lower risk of accidents occurring at the installations involved in the reprocessing of spent fuel because they process smaller amounts of radioactive waste.

The issues concerning reprocessing of spent fuel have caused a strong reaction among German society. The intensity of the protests has been addressed in the FCC's judgement concerning a sit-in organised to stop the construction of the spent fuel processing installation in Wackersdorf.[238]

Radioactive radiation has its source not only in high-capacity commercial nuclear reactors but also in the many nuclear reactors used for research purposes, operating at medium capacity. At present, the spent fuel generated by these reactors is neutralised in the countries of its origin. It is temporarily stored in Germany until it is transported to a disposal site.[239]

6. Regulation on protection against the effects of ionising radiation

The Federal Government adopted a new regulation on protection against the effects of ionising radiation (*Strahlenschutzverordnung*) on 29 November 2018. This type of regulation, according to Article 80(2) of *Grundgesetz*, requires the consent of the Bundesrat. If the Bundestag and Bundesrat disagree, joint committees are usually appointed to work out a joint compromise text for federal laws. For example, in the case of the previously effective *Strahlenschutzverordnung* of 20 July 2001, the Bundesrat only gave its consent after ca. 90 amendments made by the Bundesrat were introduced.[240]

The scope of the *Strahlenschutzverordnung* (of 2018) covers the following areas: (a) the handling of radioactive material (both of natural and artificial origin), including the acquisition, donation, domestic and international transport of such material; (b) building permits; (c) the exemption from nuclear law regulation of specified radioactive material or contaminated movable or immovable property; (d) the protection of persons exposed to radiation in the course of their occupation; (e) the performance of activities specified in Atomic Law (storage, treatment and other management of nuclear fuel), as well as the operation of nuclear installations (commercial and research reactors) and the nuclear installation of a perpetual storage facility for radioactive waste, (f) installations for the production of ionising radiation; (g) the addition of radioactive material during the manufacture of consumer goods, medicines, plant protection products, etc. The broad regulatory scope of *Strahlenschutzverordnung* best demonstrates that radiation protection is not only related to the generation of electricity in nuclear reactors, but applies to many technical and medical devices.

One of the key regulations for the nuclear power industry are the provisions of Chapter 3 of *Strahlenschutzverordnung*, which concerns the regulation of the status of infrastructure previously used at a particular nuclear installation after its decontamination (*Freigabe*). A *Freigabe* is an administrative act by which specific radioactive material or contaminated movable property, buildings, land or equipment is exempt from nuclear or radiation protection regulation. A necessary condition under the first sentence of §29(2) of *Strahlenschutzverordnung* is that the level of radiation must not exceed 10 millisieverts per person per calendar year. In the case of *Freigabe*, this refers to the recycling of materials which were used in the operation of the respective nuclear power plant or other nuclear installations.[241] Otherwise, the infrastructure of the nuclear installations concerned remains subject to the specific regulatory regime of nuclear law.

Among the provisions concerning the protection of persons occupationally exposed to radiation whose source is not related to nuclear installations or to the use of radioactive material, attention should be drawn to the regulation concerning pilots as well as cabin crew. According to §71(2) of *Strahlenschutzverordnung*, the level of exposure to cosmic radiation of cabin crew must not exceed 6 millisieverts per calendar year. The employer is obliged to minimise the level of radiation to which a person is exposed. It is worth pointing out that the 2001 regulation allowed for an exposure of 20 millisieverts per calendar year. On the other hand, the total exposure of each person during his or her working life must not exceed 100 millisieverts (§74(1)). This level was set at twice the level of the 2001 regulation. Currently, only volunteers may be exposed to more than 100 millisieverts over a lifetime (§74(2)).

7. Decommissioning and decontamination of nuclear installations

Nuclear waste in the form of spent fuel is only part of the problem associated with radioactive material. Another important and equally problematic element is the technical infrastructure that remains after its use as a nuclear installation has ended. The decontamination of disused nuclear installations is as important a process as safeguarding the radioactive waste that has already been generated. At the same time, further radioactive waste is generated in connection with the disposal of the infrastructure left behind by the nuclear installations.

The process of securing infrastructure is referred to as nuclear decommissioning. It comprises all measures and actions taken after the final shutdown of the generating activity of a nuclear installation to achieve one of three objectives.[242] First, this objective may be the decommissioning of the nuclear installation concerned.[243] This includes demolishing the buildings, exempting the occupied site from the application of Atomic Law and achieving a *greenfield* status.[244] The second possible objective to be achieved in connection with decommissioning is to achieve such a state of safety of the given installation (after its decontamination) that will enable its normal use (for other than nuclear purposes). The decontamination process ends with the removal of the installation from the scope of application of Atomic Law.[245] A third option is the continued use of the facility in question as an installation subject to Atomic Law.[246] In order to carry out the decontamination process in an orderly manner, the Radioactive Waste Disposal Commission (*Entsorgungskommission)* has drawn up appropriate guidelines.[247]

Decommissioning has only been completed for three commercial reactors (as of December 2019).[248] These have been exempted from the regulation of Atomic Law.[249] In addition, one commercial nuclear reactor was in the process of definitive cessation of production, but the administrative decision to shut it down has not yet been issued.[250] As for a further 25 commercial nuclear reactors, the administrative decisions of shutting them down have been issued.[251]

The decontamination of research reactors is proceeding much more efficiently. Decommissioning has been completed for 31 such reactors.[252] These have been exempted from the regulation of Atomic Law.[253] Five research reactors have been definitively shut down but are awaiting decommissioning administrative decisions,[254] while a further six were in the process of definitive cessation of production, but the administrative decision to shut them down has not yet been issued.[255]

Presenting the legal framework related to the decommissioning and decontamination of nuclear installations, and then contrasting it with the actual processes of decommissioning and decontamination of different types of nuclear installations serves to show the functioning of the constitutional standard "the polluter pays". Once the use of nuclear installations has been terminated, an orderly end to the process is required along with the restoration of the original state, i.e. free of radiation sources. The slow progress in this area in Germany shows what a great technical challenge this poses and thus how much of a burden this constitutional standard entails for nuclear operators. At the same time, the phase of shutdown and decontamination of nuclear installations represents the final stage in the life cycle of nuclear installations, so the extent of the burden of shutdown and decontamination that awaits each nuclear installation operator at the end should be taken into account when authorising its construction and operation, on a par with the issue of radioactive waste that will remain after each nuclear installation.

Notes

1 M.Rodi, *Grundlagen und Entwicklungslinien des Atomrechts*, "NJW" 2000, p. 12.

2 A.Brunnengräber, *The wicked problem of long term radioactive waste governance* [in:] A.Brunnengräber, M.Di Nucci (eds.), *Conflicts, participation and acceptability in nuclear waste governance*, Wiesbaden 2019, p. 339.

3 Ibid.
4 J.Kuhbier, U.Prall, *Errichtung und Betrieb von Endlagern für radioaktive Abfälle durch Beliehene?*, "ZUR" 2009, vol. 7–8, p. 359.
5 O.Däuper, A.Bernstorff, *Gesetz zur Suche und Auswahl eines Standortes für die Endlagerung radioaktiver Abfälle – zugleich ein Vorschlag für die Agenda der "Kommission Lagerung hoch radioaktiver Abfallstoffe"*, "ZUR" 2014, p. 24.
6 B.Bonin, *Jak postępować z odpadami jądrowymi?* [in:] K.Jeleń, Z.Rau (eds.), *Energetyka jądrowa w Polsce*, Warsaw 2012, p. 684.
7 O.Däuper, A.Bernstorff, *Gesetz* . . . , p. 24. See also: Referat RS III 3 *Betrieb der Verglasungseinrichtung Karlsruhe (VEK) genehmigt*, "Umwelt" 2009, issue 4, p. 310.
8 J.Kuhbier, U.Prall, *Errichtung* . . . , p. 359.
9 Ibid.
10 A.Hollenbach, *Nukleare Nachsorge – Gefahrenabwehr auf Grund des Atomrechts oder des allgemeinen Polizeirechts?*, "NVwZ" 2008, p. 1065.
11 Ibid.
12 H.Haedrich, *Zur Zulässigkeit der Wiederaufarbeitung abgebrannter Brennelemente aus deutschen Kernkraftwerken in anderen EG-Mitgliedstaaten*, "NVwZ" 1993, p. 1038.
13 L.Knopp, *Die "radioaktive" Altlast*, "NVwZ" 1991, p. 42.
14 M.Ramana, *Why technical solutions are insufficient. The abiding conundrum of nuclear waste* [in:] A.Brunnengräber, M.Di Nucci (eds.), *Conflicts* . . . , p. 32.
15 Z.Celiński [in:] J.Wojnowski (ed.), *Wielka Encyklopedia PWN*, vol. 22, Warsaw 2004, p. 342.
16 Judgement of the Higher Regional Court (Oberlandsgericht) in Celle of 9 December 1986, ref. no. I Ss 434/86, publication: "Neue Juristische Wochenschrift" 1987, p. 1281.
17 As the currently binding *Strahlenschutzverordnung* ordinance of 29 November 2018 does not contain such a clear definition of radioactive waste, the previously binding normative definition was presented.
18 L.Knopp, *Die "radioaktive"* . . . , p. 43.
19 *OVG Lüneburg: Zwischenlager für abgebrannte Brennelemente und schwachradioaktive Abfälle*, "NVwZ" 1982, p. 258.
20 See: L.Knopp, *Die "radioaktive"* . . . , p. 43 et seq.
21 Ibid., p. 45.
22 Ibid.
23 H.Wagner, *Das neue Strahlenschutzrecht*, "NVwZ" 2002, p. 172.
24 C.Degenhart, *Staatsrecht I: Staatszielbestimmungen, Staatsorgane, Staatsfunktionen*, Heidelberg 1997, p. 40.
25 T.Maunz, R.Zippelius, *Deutsches Staatsrecht*, München 1994, p. 310.
26 J.Schwabe, *Grundkurs Staatsrecht*, Berlin 1995, p. 48.
27 Judgement of the Higher Regional Court (Oberlandsgericht) in Celle of 9 December 1986, ref. no. I Ss 434/86, publication: *Oberlandsgericht Celle, Urteil vom 9.12.1986 – I Ss 434/86*, "Neue Juristische Wochenschrift" 1987, p. 1281.
28 M.Heintzen, *Commentary to Art. 73* [in:] H.von Mangoldt, F.Klein, Ch.Starck (eds.), *Kommentar zum Grundgesetz*, München 2010, §135.
29 A.Uhle, *Commentary to Art. 73* [in:] T.Maunz, G.Dürig (eds.), *Grundgesetz. Loseblatt-Kommentar*, München 2015, p. 273. The author refers there to the encyclopaedic entry for "radioactivity".
30 J.Wojnowski (ed.), *Wielka Encyklopedia PWN*, vol. 19, Warsaw 2003, p. 219.

31 A.Uhle, *Commentary . . .*, p. 273.
32 J.Żylicz [in:] J.Wojnowski (ed.), *Wielka Encyklopedia PWN*, vol. 22, Warsaw 2004, p. 342.
33 P.Kunig [in:] P.Kunig (ed.), *Grundgesetz-Kommentar*, München 1996, p. 102.
34 H.Junker, *Commentary to §§2–2b AtG* [in:] W.Danner, C.Theobald (eds.), *Energierecht*, vol. 3, München 2015, §3.
35 Ibid.
36 H.Junker, *Commentary to §§2–2b AtG . . .*, §4.
37 Ibid.
38 W.Bischof, *Commentary to Art. 74 item 11a* [in:] R.Dolzer, K.Vogel, *Bonner Kommentar zum Grundgesetz*, Heidelberg 1994, p. 74.
39 H.Junker, *Commentary to §§2–2b AtG . . .* §2; A.Uhle, *Commentary to Art. 73 . . .*, p. 273.
40 A.Uhle, *Commentary . . .*, p. 273.
41 Ibid.
42 W.Bischof, *Commentary . . .*, p. 23.
43 Ibid.
44 Ibid.
45 Ibid.
46 K.Schnapauff [in:] D.Hömig (ed.), *Grundgesetz . . .*, p. 502.
47 P.Kunig [in:] P.Kunig (ed.), *Grundgesetz . . .*, p. 103.
48 Ibid.
49 Ibid.
50 BVerfGE104,238, p. 249. See also: A.Uhle, *Commentary . . .*, p. 274.
51 K.Schnapauff [in:] D.Hömig (ed.), *Grundgesetz . . .*, p. 502.
52 According to Article 3 item 3 of the Council Directive 2011/70/EURATOM of 19 July 2011 establishing a Community framework for the responsible and safe management of spent fuel and radioactive waste, the term actually used is "disposal".
53 Ibid.
54 A.Uhle, *Commentary . . .*, p. 274.
55 Ibid.
56 Ibid.
57 Ibid.
58 C.Koenig, *Das Verbot der Abgabe von Kernbrennstoffen gemäß §9a I 2 AtG auf dem Prüfstein des Gemeinschaftsrechts*, "Europäische Zeitschrift für Wirtschaftsrecht" 2007, p. 139.
59 K.Madaj, *50 lat postępowania z odpadami promieniotwórczymi w Polsce* [in:] K.Jeleń, Z.Rau (eds.), *Energetyka jądrowa w Polsce*, Warsaw 2012, p. 890.
60 K.Madaj, *50 lat . . .*, p. 891.
61 See: Chapter III.
62 B.Bonin, *Jak postępować . . .*, p. 690.
63 G.Hammond, *Nuclear power in the twenty-first century* [in:] I.Galarraga, M.Gonzalez-Eguino, A.Markandya (eds.), *Handbook of sustainable energy*, Northampton 2011, p. 334.
64 A.Brunnengräber, *The wicked problem . . .*, p. 344.
65 C.Offermann, *Die Entsorgung radioaktiver Abfälle eine Stellungnahme zum Entsorgungsbericht'88*, "NVwZ" 1989, p. 1120.
66 C.Offermann, *Die Entsorgung . . .*, p. 1120; B.Bonin, *Jak postępować . . .*, p. 687; J.Niewodniczański, *Wprowadzenie do energetyki jądrowej* [in:] K.Jeleń, Z.Rau (eds.), *Energetyka jądrowa w Polsce*, Warsaw 2012, p. 49.

67 B.Bonin, *Jak postępować* . . . , p. 687.
68 Ibid.
69 C.Offermann, *Die Entsorgung* . . . , p. 1119.
70 B.Bonin, *Jak postępować* . . . , p. 687.
71 See: rationale for the act, p. 63.
72 The technical feasibility of reversibility and possible recovery of permanently stored radioactive waste is still a matter of discussion.
73 See: FCC's judgement of 12 November 2008, ref. no. 1 BvR 2456/06.
74 Ibid., §36. Article 2 (2) sentence 1 of the German Constitution reads as follows: "Every person shall have the right to life and physical integrity".
75 See: FCC's judgement of 12 November 2008, ref. no. 1 BvR 2456/06, §36.
76 Ibid., §37.
77 Ibid., §36.
78 FCC's judgement of 8 August 1978, publ. BVerfGE49,89.
79 See: FCC's judgement of 12 November 2008, ref. no. 1 BvR 2456/06, §37; earlier judicial decisions: BVerfGE53,30, p. 56 et seq.
80 Cf. FCC's judgement of 12 November 2008, ref. no. 1 BvR 2456/06, §37.
81 Ibid., §37.
82 K.Schnapauff [in:] D.Hömig (ed.), *Grundgesetz* . . . , p. 502; A.Uhle, *Commentary* . . . , p. 273.
83 Ibid.
84 W.Bischof, *Commentary* . . . , p. 23.
85 B.Pieroth [in:] H.Jarass, B.Pieroth (eds.), *Grundgesetz für die Bundesrepublik Deutschland. Kommentar*, München 2004, p. 905. Likewise: P.Kunig [in:] P.Kunig (ed.), *Grundgesetz* . . . , p. 102; A.Uhle, *Commentary* . . . , p. 271.
86 B.Schmidt-Bleibtreu [in:] B.Schmidt-Bleibtreu, F.Klein (eds.), *Kommentar zum Grundgesetz*, Berlin 1995, p. 987.
87 Ibid.
88 Ibid.
89 Ibid.
90 A.Uhle, *Commentary* . . . , p. 272.
91 Ibid.
92 Ibid.
93 Ibid.
94 Ibid., p. 273.
95 See also: A.Hollenbach, *Nukleare* . . . , pp. 1065 and 1069.
96 See: H.Kushner, *Encyclopedia of terrorism*, Thousand Oaks 2003, pp. 264–265.
97 A.Hollenbach, *Nukleare* . . . , p. 1069.
98 H.Kushner, *Encyclopedia* . . . , pp. 263–264.
99 Ibid., p. 264.
100 P.Kunig [in:] P.Kunig (ed.), *Grundgesetz* . . . , p. 102; A.Uhle, *Commentary* . . . , p. 271.
101 A.Uhle, *Commentary* . . . , p. 271.
102 Ibid.
103 Ibid.
104 B.Schmidt-Bleibtreu [in:] B.Schmidt-Bleibtreu, F.Klein, *Kommentar* . . . , p. 987; cf. also: P.Kunig [in:] P.Kunig (ed.), *Grundgesetz* . . . , p. 101.
105 A.Uhle, *Commentary* . . . , p. 272.
106 Ibid.
107 Ibid.

108 C.Offermann, *Die Entsorgung . . .* , p. 1112.
109 A.Uhle, *Commentary to Art. 73 . . .* , p. 272.
110 See: Chapter III.
111 M.Rodi, *Grundlagen . . .* , p. 11.
112 H.Haedrich, *Zur Zulässigkeit . . .* , p. 1037; F.Matthes, *Stromwirtschaft und deutsche Einheit. Eine Fallstudie zur Transformation der Elektrizitätswirtschaft in Ost-Deutschland*, Berlin 2000, p. 148. See also: *OVG Lüneburg: Zwischenlager für abgebrannte Brennelemente und schwach-radioaktive Abfälle*, "NVwZ" 1982, p. 258.
113 F.Matthes, *Stromwirtschaft . . .* , p. 148.
114 A.Tiggemann, *The elephant in the room. The role of Gorleben and its site selection in the German nuclear waste debate* [in:] A.Brunnengräber, M.Di Nucci (eds.), *Conflicts . . .* , p. 72.
115 M.Schüring, *"Bekennen gegen den Atomstaat". Historische und religiöse Codierungen im kirchlichen Protest gegen die Atomenergie in den 70er und 80er Jahren* [in:] J.Ostheimer, M.Vogt (eds.), *Die Moral der Energiewende. Risikowahrnehmung im Wandel am Beispiel der Atomenergie*, Stuttgart 2014, p. 241.
116 F.Matthes, *Stromwirtschaft . . .* , p. 148.
117 H.Haedrich, *Zur Zulässigkeit . . .* , p. 1037.
118 BVerfGE104,238, pp. 239–240.
119 BVerfGE104,238, p. 240.
120 Bundesminister des Innern, *Antwort der Bundesregierung auf die Große Anfrage der Abgeordneten Dr. Laufs, Dr. Dregger, Spranger, Dr. Riesenhuber, Dr. Miltner, Lenzer, Broll, Fellner, Dr. von Geldern, Gerlach, Dr. Waffenschmidt, Dr. Bugl, Gerstein, Frau Hürland, Kolb, Dr. George, Dr. Jobst, Dr. Köhler (Wolfsburg), Dr. Kunz (Weiden), Magin, Pfeffermann, Prangenberg, Schwarz, Dr. Stavenhagen und der Fraktion der CDU/CSU – Drucksache 9/858 – Verantwortung des Bundes für Sicherstellung und Endlagerung radioaktiver Abfälle in der Bundesrepublik Deutschland* of 22 December 1981, publication: "Deutscher Bundestag Drucksache 9/1231", p. 3.
121 A.Tiggemann, *The elephant . . .* , pp. 75–76; F.Matthes, *Stromwirtschaft . . .* , p. 148; H.Wagner, *Ist das Atomgesetz verfassungswidrig?*, "NJW" 1989, p. 1828.
122 It was the act of 30 August 1976. Publ. BGBl I, 2573.
123 P.Becker, *Aufstieg und Krise der deutschen Stromkonzerne*, Bochum 2011, p. 208.
124 Ibid.
125 C.Salander, *The present status of "Entsorgung" for nuclear power plants in the Federal Republic of Germany* [w:] K.Kaiser (red.), *Reconciling energy . . .* , p. 72; O.Däuper, K.Bosch, R.Ringwald, *Zur Finanzierung des Standortauswahlverfahrens für ein atomares Endlager durch Beiträge der Abfallverursacher*, „ZUR" 2013, p. 330.
126 A.Tiggemann, *The elephant . . .* , p. 75–76.
127 M.Rodi, *Grundlagen . . .* , pp. 11–12.
128 M.Ramana, *Why technical solutions . . .* , p. 27; C.Drögemüller, *Schlüsselakteure der Endlager-Governance. Entsorgungsoptionen und – strategien radioaktiver Abfälle aus Sicht regionaler Akteure*, Wiesbaden 2018, p. 2.
129 P.Batista, *The debate on reprocessing* [in:] K.Kaiser (ed.), *Reconciling energy . . .* , p. 58.

130 B.Bonin, *Jak postępować . . .* , p. 686 et seq.
131 Ibid., p. 686.
132 The division was proposed by C. Offermann in *Die Entsorgung. . . .* , p. 1118.
133 M.Häberle, *Commentary to §9a AtomG*, §2 [in:] G.Erbs, M.Kohlhaas (reds.), *Strafrechtliche Nebengesetze mit Straf- und Bußgeldvorschriften des Wirtschafts- und Verwaltungsrechts*, vol. 1, München 2015; C.Offermann, *Die Entsorgung . . .* , p. 1119; H.Wagner, *30 Jahre Atomgesetz – 30 Jahre Umweltschutz*, "NVwZ" 1989, p. 1110; H.Wagner, *Ist das Atomgesetz . . .* , p. 1828.
134 BVerfGE104,238, p. 239.
135 C.Offermann, *Die Entsorgung . . .* , p. 1112.
136 *Übereinkommen über nukleare Sicherheit. Bericht der Bundesrepublik Deutschland für die Sechste Überprüfungstagung im März/April 2014*, Bonn 2013, p. 178.
137 C.Offermann, *Die Entsorgung . . .* , p. 1116.
138 Publ. BGBl. I p. 1618.
139 BVerfGE104,238, p. 241.
140 Cf. A.Roßnagel, *Radioaktiver Zerfall der Grundrechte? Zur Verfassungsverträglichkeit der Kernenergie*, Monachium 1984; C.Salander, *The present status of "Entsorgung" for nuclear power plants in the Federal Republic of Germany* [in:] K.Kaiser (ed.), *Reconciling energy . . .* , p. 71 et seq.; P.Batista, *The debate on reprocessing* [in:] K.Kaiser (ed.), *Reconciling energy needs and non-proliferation. Perspectives on nuclear technology . . .* , sp. 55 et seq.; S.Eklung, *Safeguarding plutonium in the global energy economy of the future: problems and prospects* [in:] K.Kaiser (ed.), *Reconciling energy . . .* , p. 77 et seq.; K.Beckurts, D.Leushacke, *Processing and enrichment. Are there alternatives which are more proliferation-proof?* [in:] K.Kaiser (ed.), *Reconciling energy . . .* , p. 82 et seq.; V.Hauff, *Reconciling energy needs and non-proliferation: a German perspective* [in:] K.Kaiser (ed.), *Reconciling energy . . .* , pp. 32–35; L.Weiss, *Reprocessing and enrichment: are there alternatives which are more proliferation-proof?* [in:] K.Kaiser (ed.), *Reconciling energy . . .* , p. 96 et seq.; H.Kouts, *Reprocessing and enrichment: their proliferation resistance* [in:] K.Kaiser (ed.), *Reconciling energy . . .* , p. 101; R.Fox, *Natural uranium and enrichment: the politics of supply and access* [in:] K.Kaiser (ed.), *Reconciling energy . . .* , p. 107 et seq.; K.Niizeki, *Natural uranium and enrichment: the politics of supply and access* [in:] K.Kaiser (ed.), *Reconciling energy . . .* , p. 120 et seq.; K.Ho Hyun, *Natural uranium and enrichment: the politics of supply and access* [in:] K.Kaiser (ed.), *Reconciling energy . . .* , p. 122 et seq.; T.Pickering, *Implementing the Nuclear Non-Proliferation Act of 1978* [in:] K.Kaiser (ed.), *Reconciling energy . . .* , p. 130 et seq.; H.Menderhausen, *The multinationalization of reprocessing and enrichment: how and where?* [in:] K.Kaiser (ed.), *Reconciling energy . . .* , p. 137 et seq.; R.Rometsch, *The multinationalization of reprocessing and enrichment: how and where?* [in:] K.Kaiser (ed.), *Reconciling energy . . .* , p. 149 et seq.; M.Osredkar, *The multinationalization of reprocessing and enrichment: how and where?* [in:] K.Kaiser (ed.), *Reconciling energy . . .* , p. 154 et seq.; H.Rowen, *Exploring nuclear futures: a statement of the issues regarding nuclear energy and proliferation* [in:] K.Kaiser (ed.), *Reconciling energy . . .* , p. 157 et seq.; J.Hill, *Driving forces of proliferation* [in:] K.Kaiser (ed.), *Reconciling energy needs and non-proliferation. Perspectives on nuclear technology and international politics*, Bonn 1980, p. 166 et seq.; G.Quester, *Diversion-resistant technologies and multinational management*

[in:] K.Kaiser (ed.), *Reconciling energy* . . . , p. 178 et seq. Critically: P.Becker, *Aufstieg und Krise der deutschen Stromkonzerne* . . . , pp. 209–212; C.Doren, *The debate on reprocessing* [in:] K.Kaiser (ed.), *Reconciling energy* . . . , p. 60 et seq.

141 P.Batista, *The debate* . . . , p. 55.
142 C.Offermann, *Die Entsorgung* . . . , p. 1114.
143 Ibid.
144 H.Wagner, *30 Jahre Atomgesetz* . . . , p. 1110.
145 P.Batista, *The debate* . . . , p. 55.
146 Ibid.
147 S.Eklung, *Safeguarding plutonium* . . . , p. 78.
148 C.Salander, *The present status* . . . , p. 71.
149 Ibid., p. 72. Critically on account of e.g. involving too high a price to pay to achieve "potential social benefits" in the future: C.Doren, *The debate* . . . , p. 60. A similar opinion about costs can be found in P.Becker's *Aufstieg* . . . , p. 211.
150 C.Offermann, *Die Entsorgung* . . . , p. 1115.
151 C.Salander, *The present status* . . . , p. 72.
152 C.Offermann, *Die Entsorgung* . . . , p. 1115.
153 Ibid., p. 1114.
154 C.Salander, *The present status* . . . , p. 72.
155 K.Ho Hyun, *Natural uranium* . . . , p. 122.
156 C.Salander, *The present status* . . . , p. 72.
157 V.Hauff, *Reconciling energy* . . . , p. 32.
158 H.Kouts, *Reprocessing* . . . , p. 104.
159 P.Batista, *The debate* . . . , p. 55.
160 K.Niizeki, *Natural uranium* . . . , p. 120.
161 K.Ho Hyun, *Natural uranium* . . . , p. 123.
162 K.Niizeki, *Natural uranium* . . . , p. 121; J.Hill, *Driving forces* . . . , p. 171. Similarly on the grounds of membership in international consortia dealing with reprocessing: M.Osredkar, *The multinationalization* . . . , pp. 154–155. Cf. in relation to the American restrictions on the export of technology, including reprocessing: C.Madero, *Driving forces of proliferation* [in:] K.Kaiser (ed.), *Reconciling energy* . . . , p. 175 et seq.
163 F.Uekötter, *Die neue Dolchstoßlegende. Fukushima und die Mythen der atomaren Geschichte* [in:] J.Ostheimer, M.Vogt (eds.), *Die Moral* . . . , p. 250.
164 P.Batista, *The debate* . . . , p. 58.
165 B.Bonin, *Jak postępować* . . . , p. 690.
166 P.Batista, *The debate* . . . , p. 58.
167 See: S.Eklung, *Safeguarding plutonium* . . . , p. 78; K.Beckurts, D.Leushacke, *Processing.* . . . , p. 82.
168 P.Batista, *The debate* . . . , pp. 55–56. Critically: J.Hill, *Driving forces* . . . , p. 173.
169 P.Batista, *The debate* . . . , p. 56.
170 Ibid.; S.Eklung, *Safeguarding plutonium* . . . , p. 78; K.Beckurts, D.Leushacke, *Processing.* . . . , p. 87.
171 C.Doren, *The debate* . . . , p. 62.
172 A.Hollenbach, *Nukleare Nachsorge* . . . , p. 1065.
173 S.Eklung, *Safeguarding plutonium* . . . , pp. 80–81.
174 H.Menderhausen, *The multinationalization* . . . , p. 137 et seq.

175 Ibid., p. 138.
176 G.Quester, *Diversion-resistant technologies . . .*, p. 180.
177 Ibid., p. 181.
178 Ibid., p. 182.
179 H.Wagner, *Ist das Atomgesetz . . .*, p. 1826.
180 C.Offermann, *Die Entsorgung . . .*, p. 1115.
181 C.Doren, *The debate . . .*, p. 62.
182 C.Offermann, *Die Entsorgung . . .*, p. 1113; Referat RS III 3 *Betrieb . . .*, p. 310.
183 F.Matthes, *Stromwirtschaft . . .*, p. 148.
184 C.Offermann, *Die Entsorgung . . .*, p. 1113.
185 F.Matthes, *Stromwirtschaft . . .*, p. 148.
186 Ibid.
187 H.Haedrich, *Zur Zulässigkeit . . .*, p. 1037.
188 Ibid. and: Bundesminister des Innern, *Antwort der Bundesregierung . . .*, p. 1.
189 H.Haedrich, *Zur Zulässigkeit . . .*, p. 1037.
190 C.Offermann, *Die Entsorgung . . .*, p. 1113. See also: J.Hofmann, *Bauplanung und Atomrecht – das Beispiel Wiederaufbereitungsanlage Wackersdorf*, "NVwZ" 1989, pp. 225–231; H.Wagner, *Ist das Atomgesetz . . .*, p. 1828; P.Becker, *Aufstieg . . .*, p. 211; FCC's judgement of 24 October 2001, ref. no. 1 BvR 1190/90, 1 BvR 2173/93, 1 BvR 433/96, publ. BVerfGE104,92; FCC's judgement of 7 June 1986, ref. no. 1 BvR 647/86, publ. BVerfGE72,299.
191 C.Offermann, *Die Entsorgung . . .*, pp. 1113–1114.
192 Ibid., p. 1114.
193 H.Haedrich, *Zur Zulässigkeit . . .*, p. 1037.
194 M.Rodi, *Grundlagen . . .*, p. 12; C.Offermann, *Die Entsorgung . . .*, p. 1114; B.Stüer, S.Schüttorf, *Ausstieg aus der Atomenergie zum Nulltarif?* "NVwZ" 2000, p. 10.
195 B.Stüer, S.Schüttorf, *Ausstieg . . .*, p. 10.
196 Ibid.
197 Referat RS III 3 *Betrieb . . .*, p. 310.
198 Ibid.
199 C.Offermann, *Die Entsorgung . . .*, p. 1115.
200 Ibid.
201 Referat RS III 3 *Betrieb . . .*, p. 310.
202 C.Offermann, *Die Entsorgung . . .*, p. 1114.
203 M.Rodi, *Grundlagen . . .*, p. 12.
204 H.Haedrich, *Zur Zulässigkeit . . .*, p. 1036.
205 M.Rodi, *Grundlagen . . .*, p. 12; H.Haedrich, *Zur Zulässigkeit . . .*, p. 1038.
206 M.Rodi, *Grundlagen . . .*, p. 12.
207 H.Haedrich, *Zur Zulässigkeit . . .*, p. 1036.
208 Ibid. and: H.Wagner, *Ist das Atomgesetz . . .*, p. 1828.
209 Similarly: H.Haedrich, *Zur Zulässigkeit . . .*, p. 148.
210 Ibid., pp. 1038–1044.
211 M.Häberle, *Commentary to §9a AtomG . . .*, §2.
212 Based on the content available in: P.Becker, *Aufstieg . . .*, p. 352.
213 Ibid.
214 M.Häberle, *Commentary to §9a AtomG . . .*, §3.
215 M.Rodi, *Grundlagen . . .*, p. 12. Against such a solution as early as in 1993: H.Haedrich, *Zur Zulässigkeit . . .*, pp. 1038–1044.

216 M.Rodi, *Grundlagen* . . . , p. 12.
217 B.Stüer, S.Schüttorf, *Ausstieg* . . . , p. 10.
218 Ibid.
219 Ibid.
220 C.Koenig, *Das Verbot* . . . , p. 139; H.Koch, A.Roβnagel, *Neue Energiepolitik und Ausstieg aus der Kernenergie*, "NVwZ" 2000, p. 8.
221 C.Koenig, *Das Verbot* . . . , p. 139.
222 See: J.Linck, *Protestaktionen gegen Castor-Transporte und das geltende Recht*, "Zeitschrift für Rechtspolitik" 2011, p. 44 et seq. From a rich body of judicial decisions: *BVerfG: Klagebefugnis von Anliegern der Beförderungsstrecke für Castor-Behälter*, "NVwZ" 2009, pp. 515–518; *BVerfG: Castor-Transport nach Gorleben*, "NJW" 2001, pp. 1411–1413; *BVerfG: Unbefugtes Betreten einer Bahnanlage bei Anti-Castor-Demonstration*, "NJW" 1998, pp. 3113–3114.
223 See: E.Bohne, M.Speyer, *Staat und Konfliktbewältigung bei Zukunftstechnologien*, "NVwZ" 1999, p. 1.
224 Bundesamt für Verfassungsschutz, *Linksextremistische/militante Bestrebungen im Rahmen der Anti-CASTOR-Kampagne. Konzepte und Gruppen (Wendland)*, Köln 1996, p. 2.
225 Bundesamt für Verfassungsschutz, *Linksextremistische/militante* . . . , pp. 2–3.
226 H.Koch, A.Roβnagel, *Neue Energiepolitik* . . . , p. 8.
227 Ibid., p. 9.
228 Ibid.
229 Ibid.
230 C.Koenig, *Das Verbot* . . . , p. 142.
231 H.Koch, A.Roβnagel, *Neue Energiepolitik* . . . , p. 8.
232 See: C.Koenig, *Das Verbot* . . . , pp. 139–144.
233 Ibid., p. 140.
234 Ibid., pp. 140–141.
235 Ibid., pp. 141–143, p. 144.
236 Ibid., pp. 143–144.
237 Ibid.
238 FCC's judgement of 24 October 2001, ref. no. 1 BvR 1190, 1 BvR 2173/93, 1 BvR 433/96, publ. BVerfGE104,92. See also: FCC's judgement of 11 November 1986, ref. no. 1 BvR 713/83, 1 BvR 921/84, 1 BvR 1190/84, 1 BvR 333/85, 1 BvR 248/85, 1 BvR 306/85, 1 BvR 497/85, publ. BVerfGE73,206. Cf. B.Rusteberg, *Die Verhinderungsblockade* "NJW" 2011, pp. 2999–3003.
239 *Übereinkommen* . . . , p. 178.
240 H.Wagner, *Das neue Strahlenschutzrecht* . . . , p. 168.
241 Ibid., p. 172.
242 Entsorgungskommission, *Empfehlung* . . . , p. 4. www.entsorgungskommission.de/sites/default/files/reports/empfllstesk46hp.pdf [Date of access: 14 May 2016].
243 Ibid.
244 Ibid.
245 Entsorgungskommission, *Empfehlung* . . . , p. 4.
246 Ibid.
247 Ibid., pp. 5 et seq.
248 Bundesamt für die Sicherheit der nuklearen Entsorgung, *Statusbericht zur Kernenergienutzung in der Bundesrepublik Deutschland 2019*, p. 28. <https://doris.bfs.de/jspui/handle/urn:nbn:de:0221-2020092123025>.

249 Ibid., p. 20.
250 Ibid., p. 21.
251 Ibid.
252 Ibid., p. 36.
253 Ibid.
254 Ibid., p. 34.
255 Ibid., p. 31.

References

BASE, *Statusbericht zur Kernenergienutzung in der Bundesrepublik Deutschland 2019*. https://doris.bfs.de/jspui/handle/urn:nbn:de:0221-2020092123025.

Batista P., *The debate on reprocessing* [in:] K.Kaiser (ed.), *Reconciling energy needs and non-proliferation. Perspectives on nuclear technology and international politics*, Bonn 1980.

Becker P., *Aufstieg und Krise der deutschen Stromkonzerne*, Bochum 2011.

Beckurts K., Leushacke D., *Processing and enrichment. Are there alternatives which are more proliferation-proof?* [in:] K.Kaiser (ed.), *Reconciling energy needs and non-proliferation. Perspectives on nuclear technology and international politics*, Bonn 1980.

Bischof W., *A Commentary to Art. 74 item 11a* [in:] R.Dolzer, K.Vogel (eds.), *Bonner Kommentar zum Grundgesetz*, Heidelberg 1994.

Bohne E., Speyer M., *Staat und Konfliktbewältigung bei Zukunftstechnologien*, "NVwZ" 1999, pp. 1–11.

Bonin B., *Jak postępować z odpadami jądrowymi?* [in:] K.Jeleń, Z.Rau (eds.), *Energetyka jądrowa w Polsce*, Warsaw 2012.

Brunnengräber A., *The wicked problem of long term radioactive waste governance* [in:] A.Brunnengräber, M.Di Nucci (eds.), *Conflicts, participation and acceptability in nuclear waste governance*, Wiesbaden 2019.

Bundesamt für Verfassungsschutz, *Linksextremistische/militante Bestrebungen im Rahmen der Anti-CASTOR-Kampagne. Konzepte und Gruppen (Wendland)*, Köln 1996.

Bundesminister des Innern, *Antwort der Bundesregierung auf die Große Anfrage der Abgeordneten Dr. Laufs, Dr. Dregger, Spranger, Dr. Riesenhuber, Dr. Miltner, Lenzer, Broll, Fellner, Dr. von Geldern, Gerlach, Dr. Waffenschmidt, Dr. Bugl, Gerstein, Frau Hürland, Kolb, Dr. George, Dr. Jobst, Dr. Köhler (Wolfsburg), Dr. Kunz (Weiden), Magin, Pfeffermann, Prangenberg, Schwarz, Dr. Stavenhagen und der Fraktion der CDU/CSU – Drucksache 9/858 – Verantwortung des Bundes für Sicherstellung und Endlagerung radioaktiver Abfälle in der Bundesrepublik Deutschland* of 22 December 1981, publication: "Deutscher Bundestag Drucksache 9/1231".

BVerfG: Castor-Transport nach Gorleben, "NJW" 2001, pp. 1411–1413.

BVerfG: Klagebefugnis von Anliegern der Beförderungsstrecke für Castor-Behälter, "NVwZ" 2009, pp. 515–518.

BVerfG: Unbefugtes Betreten einer Bahnanlage bei Anti-Castor-Demonstration, "NJW" 1998, pp. 3113–3114.

Celiński Z. [in:] J.Wojnowski (ed.), *Wielka Encyklopedia PWN*, vol. 22, Warsaw 2004, p. 342.

Däuper O., Bernstorff A., *Gesetz zur Suche und Auswahl eines Standortes für die Endlagerung radioaktiver Abfälle – zugleich ein Vorschlag für die Agenda der „Kommission Lagerung hoch radioaktiver Abfallstoffe"*, „ZUR" 2014, pp. 24–32.

Däuper O., Bosch K., Ringwald R., *Zur Finanzierung des Standortauswahlverfahrens für ein atomares Endlager durch Beiträge der Abfallverursacher*, „ZUR" 2013, pp. 329–336.

Degenhart C., *Staatsrecht I: Staatszielbestimmungen, Staatsorgane, Staatsfunktionen*, Heidelberg 1997.

Doren C., *The debate on reprocessing* [in:] K.Kaiser (ed.), *Reconciling energy needs and non-proliferation. Perspectives on nuclear technology and international politics*, Bonn 1980.

Drögemüller C., *Schlüsselakteure der Endlager-Governance. Entsorgungsoptionen und – strategien radioaktiver Abfälle aus Sicht regionaler Akteure*, Wiesbaden 2018.

Eklung S., *Safeguarding plutonium in the global energy economy of the future: problems and prospects* [in:] K.Kaiser (ed.), *Reconciling energy needs and non-proliferation. Perspectives on nuclear technology and international politics*, Bonn 1980.

Entsorgungskommission, *Empfehlung der Entsorgungskommission vom 16.03.2015. Leitlinien zur Stilllegung kerntechnischer Anlagen*. www.entsorgungskommission.de/sites/default/files/reports/empfllstesk46hp.pdf.

Fox R., *Natural uranium and enrichment: the politics of supply and access* [in:] K.Kaiser (ed.), *Reconciling energy needs and non-proliferation. Perspectives on nuclear technology and international politics*, Bonn 1980.

Häberle M., *A Commentary to §9a AtomG*, § 2 [in:] G.Erbs, M.Kohlhaas (red.), *Strafrechtliche Nebengesetze mit Straf- und Bußgeldvorschriften des Wirtschafts- und Verwaltungsrechts*, vol. 1, München 2015.

Haedrich H., *Zur Zulässigkeit der Wiederaufarbeitung abgebrannter Brennelemente aus deutschen Kernkraftwerken in anderen EG-Mitgliedstaaten*, „NVwZ" 1993, pp. 1036–1044.

Hammond G., *Nuclear power in the twenty-first century* [in:] I.Galarraga, M.Gonzalez-Eguino, A.Markandya (eds.), *Handbook of sustainable energy*, Northampton 2011.

Hauff V., *Reconciling energy needs and non-proliferation: a German perspective* [in:] K.Kaiser (ed.), *Reconciling energy needs and non-proliferation. Perspectives on nuclear technology and international politics*, Bonn 1980.

Heintzen M., *A Commentary to Art. 73* [in:] von Mangoldt H., Klein F., Starck Ch. (eds.), *Kommentar zum Grundgesetz*, München 2010.

Hill J., *Driving forces of proliferation* [in:] K.Kaiser (ed.), *Reconciling energy needs and non-proliferation. Perspectives on nuclear technology and international politics*, Bonn 1980.

Hofmann J., *Bauplanung und Atomrecht – das Beispiel Wiederaufbereitungsanlage Wackersdorf*, "NVwZ" 1989, pp. 225–231.

Ho Hyun K., *Natural uranium and enrichment: the politics of supply and access* [in:] K.Kaiser (ed.), *Reconciling energy needs and non-proliferation. Perspectives on nuclear technology and international politics*, Bonn 1980.

Hollenbach A., *Nukleare Nachsorge – Gefahrenabwehr auf Grund des Atomrechts oder des allgemeinen Polizeirechts?*, „NVwZ" 2008, p. 1065 et seq.

Jarass H., Pieroth B., *Grundgesetz für die Bundesrepublik Deutschland. Kommentar*, München 2004.

Junker H., *A Commentary to §§2–2b AtG* [in:] W.Danner, C.Theobald (eds.), *Energierecht*, vol. 3, München 2015.

Knopp L., *Die „radioaktive" Altlast*, „NVwZ" 1991, pp. 42–45.

Koch H., Roβnagel A., *Neue Energiepolitik und Ausstieg aus der Kernenergie*, "NVwZ" 2000, p. 1 et seq.

Koenig C., *Das Verbot der Abgabe von Kernbrennstoffen gemäβ § 9a I 2 AtG auf dem Prüfstein des Gemeinschaftsrechts*, "Europäische Zeitschrift für Wirtschaftsrecht" 2007, pp.

Kouts H., *Reprocessing and enrichment: their proliferation resistance* [in:] K.Kaiser (ed.), *Reconciling energy needs and non-proliferation. Perspectives on nuclear technology and international politics*, Bonn 1980.

Kuhbier J., Prall U., *Errichtung und Betrieb von Endlagern für radioaktive Abfälle durch Beliehene?*, „ZUR" 2009, No. 7–8, pp. 358–364.

Kunig P. (ed.), *Grundgesetz-Kommentar*, München 1996.

Kushner H., *Encyclopedia of terrorism*, Thousand Oaks 2003.

Linck J., *Protestaktionen gegen Castor-Transporte und das geltende Recht*, "Zeitschrift für Rechtspolitik" 2011, p. 44–46.

Madaj K., *50 lat postępowania z odpadami promieniotwórczymi w Polsce* [in:] K.Jeleń, Z.Rau (eds.), *Energetyka jądrowa w Polsce*, Warsaw 2012.

Madero C., *Driving forces of proliferation* [in:] K.Kaiser (ed.), *Reconciling energy needs and non-proliferation. Perspectives on nuclear technology and international politics*, Bonn 1980.

Matthes F., *Stromwirtschaft und deutsche Einheit. Eine Fallstudie zur Transformation der Elektrizitätswirtschaft in Ost-Deutschland*, Berlin 2000.

Maunz T., Zippelius R., *Deutsches Staatsrecht*, München 1994.

Menderhausen H., *The multinationalization of reprocessing and enrichment: how and where?* [in:] K.Kaiser (ed.), *Reconciling energy needs and non-proliferation. Perspectives on nuclear technology and international politics*, Bonn 1980.

Niewodniczański J., *Wprowadzenie do energetyki jądrowej* [in:] K.Jeleń, Z.Rau (eds.), *Energetyka jądrowa w Polsce*, Warsaw 2012.

Niizeki K., *Natural uranium and enrichment: the politics of supply and access* [in:] K.Kaiser (ed.), *Reconciling energy needs and non-proliferation. Perspectives on nuclear technology and international politics*, Bonn 1980.

Oberlandsgericht Celle, Urteil vom 9.12.1986 – I Ss 434/86, „NJW" 1987, pp. 1281–1282.

Offermann C., *Die Entsorgung radioaktiver Abfälle eine Stellungnahme zum Entsorgungsbericht'88*, "NVwZ" 1989, pp. 1112–1120.

Osredkar M., *The multinationalization of reprocessing and enrichment: how and where?* [in:] K.Kaiser (ed.), *Reconciling energy needs and non-proliferation. Perspectives on nuclear technology and international politics*, Bonn 1980.

OVG Lüneburg: Zwischenlager für abgebrannte Brennelemente und schwachradioaktive Abfälle, „NVwZ" 1982, pp. 256–263.

Pickering T., *Implementing the Nuclear Non-Proliferation Act of 1978* [in:] K.Kaiser (ed.), *Reconciling energy needs and non-proliferation. Perspectives on nuclear technology and international politics*, Bonn 1980.

Quester G., *Diversion-resistant technologies and multinational management* [in:] K.Kaiser (ed.), *Reconciling energy needs and non-proliferation. Perspectives on nuclear technology and international politics*, Bonn 1980.

Ramana M., *Why technical solutions are insufficient. The abiding conundrum of nuclear waste* [in:] A.Brunnengräber, M.Di Nucci (eds.), *Conflicts, participation and acceptability in nuclear waste governance*, Wiesbaden 2019.

Referat RS III 3, *Betrieb der Verglasungseinrichtung Karlsruhe (VEK) genehmigt*, „Umwelt" 2009, No. 4, pp. 310–311.

Rodi M., *Grundlagen und Entwicklungslinien des Atomrechts*, „NJW" 2000, p. 7 et seq.

Rometsch R., *The multinationalization of reprocessing and enrichment: how and where?* [in:] K.Kaiser (ed.), *Reconciling energy needs and non-proliferation. Perspectives on nuclear technology and international politics*, Bonn 1980.

Roßnagel A., *Radioaktiver Zerfall der Grundrechte? Zur Verfassungsverträglichkeit der Kernenergie*, München 1984.

Rowen H., *Exploring nuclear futures: a statement of the issues regarding nuclear energy and proliferation* [in:] K.Kaiser (ed.), *Reconciling energy needs and non-proliferation. Perspectives on nuclear technology and international politics*, Bonn 1980.

Rusteberg B., *Die Verhinderungsblockade* "NJW" 2011, pp. 2999–3003.

Salander C., *The present status of "Entsorgung" for nuclear power plants in the Federal Republic of Germany* [w:] K.Kaiser (ed.), *Reconciling energy needs and non-proliferation. Perspectives on nuclear technology and international politics*, Bonn 1980.

Schmidt-Bleibtreu B., Klein F., *Kommentar zum Grundgesetz*, Berlin 1995.

Schnapauff K. [in:] D.Hömig (ed.), *Grundgesetz für die Bundesrepublik Deutschland. Handkommentar*, Baden-Baden 2013.

Schüring M., *"Bekennen gegen den Atomstaat". Historische und religiöse Codierungen im kirchlichen Protest gegen die Atomenergie in den 70er und 80er Jahren* [in:] J.Ostheimer, M.Vogt (eds.), *Die Moral der Energiewende. Risikowahrnehmung im Wandel am Beispiel der Atomenergie*, Stuttgart 2014.

Schwabe J., *Grundkurs Staatsrecht*, Berlin 1995.

Stüer B., Schüttorf S., *Ausstieg aus der Atomenergie zum Nulltarif?* "NVwZ" 2000, pp. 9–15.

Tiggemann A., *The elephant in the room. The role of Gorleben and its site selection in the German nuclear waste debate* [in:] A.Brunnengräber, M.Di Nucci (eds.), *Conflicts, participation and acceptability in nuclear waste governance*, Wiesbaden 2019.

Übereinkommen über nukleare Sicherheit. Bericht der Bundesrepublik Deutschland für die Sechste Überprüfungstagung im März/April 2014, Bonn 2013.

Uekötter F., *Die neue Dolchstoßlegende. Fukushima und die Mythen der atomaren Geschichte* [in:] J.Ostheimer, M.Vogt (eds.), *Die Moral der Energiewende. Risikowahrnehmung im Wandel am Beispiel der Atomenergie*, Stuttgart 2014.

Uhle A., *A Commentary to Art. 73* [in:] T.Maunz, G.Dürig (eds.), *Grundgesetz. Loseblatt-Kommentar*, München 2015.

Wagner H., *30 Jahre Atomgesetz – 30 Jahre Umweltschutz*, „NVwZ" 1989, p. 1105 et seq.

Wagner H., *Das neue Strahlenschutzrecht*, „NVwZ" 2002, pp. 168–173.

Wagner H., *Ist das Atomgesetz verfassungswidrig?*, "NJW" 1989, p. 1825 et seq.

Weiss L., *Reprocessing and enrichment: are there alternatives which are more proliferation-proof?* [in:] K.Kaiser (ed.), *Reconciling energy needs and non-proliferation. Perspectives on nuclear technology and international politics*, Bonn 1980.

Wojnowski J. (ed.), *Wielka Encyklopedia PWN*, vol. 19, Warsaw 2003.

Wojnowski J. (ed.), *Wielka Encyklopedia PWN*, vol. 22, Warsaw 2004.

2 Storage and disposal of radioactive waste

The constitutional regulation on nuclear energy adopted in the 1950s also covered the storage of radioactive waste. Since 1965, work has been going on in Germany to establish a final disposal facility for radioactive waste.[1] However, no such repository for high-level radioactive waste has been built to date in Germany or globally.[2] Moreover, no final storage facility for non-high-level radioactive waste has yet been operating anywhere else in the world.[3]

The management of radioactive waste (particularly high-level radioactive waste) is a constant social and technical challenge. The construction of a radioactive waste disposal facility is a challenge not only technically, but also politically[4] – thus legally and constitutionally. At the same time, as a task for the German state,[5] it can only be solved in cooperation between the Federation and the Länder.[6]

It is also pointed out that as long as the issue of radioactive waste has not been resolved, it will continue to violate the constitutional principle of environmental protection.[7] Due to the lack of solutions for the management and disposal of radioactive waste, the use of nuclear power in Germany on an industrial scale is sometimes referred to in the literature as flying with your eyes closed (*Blindflug*).[8] The determination to solve this problem can be demonstrated by the fact that in the late 1970s and early 1980s, Germany was working on starting to dump weak radioactive waste on the bottom of the Atlantic Ocean on an industrial scale.[9]

1. The Länder's obligation to temporarily store radioactive waste

According to §9a(2), sentence 1 of Atomic Law, an entity that possesses radioactive waste is obliged to deliver it to an interim storage facility (*Zwischenlager*). However, interim storage facilities are only a temporary solution, due to the lack of a final storage facility for radioactive

DOI: 10.4324/9781003198086-3

waste.[10] The literature also points to another purpose for interim radioactive waste disposal facilities. The idea is to store spent nuclear fuel for several decades to reduce the amount of heat released by this highly radioactive waste before it is disposed of permanently.[11] At the same time, there is no predetermined duration for the operation of interim storage facilities.[12] The limits of their operation will be set by the establishment of a permanent radioactive waste disposal facility, one for the whole Federation, for both low- and high-level waste, followed by its safe transport to the final disposal facilities. Until then, the amount of radioactive waste stored above ground in interim storage facilities will only increase.[13]

The operation of an interim storage facility pursuant to the first sentence of §9a(3) of Atomic Law is the responsibility of each Land. The Radiation Protection Ordinance (*Strahlenschutzverordnung*) provides, however, that the transfer of radioactive waste to interim storage facilities within a Land is permissible only if the competent authority has given its consent.[14] In the absence of such consent, nuclear reactor operators are obliged to store the waste temporarily themselves. This will continue until an order is formulated to transfer it to a disposal facility.[15]

It should be noted that interim storage is not technically the same as final disposal of radioactive waste.[16] In interim storage facilities, radioactive waste is stored for extended periods of time in a form that enables it to be transferred immediately to its final storage.[17] Once vitrified,[18] high-level radioactive waste is placed in steel casks. Low- and intermediate-level radioactive waste is normally embedded in cement and also stored in steel casks.[19]

Temporary storage (on the ground) does not provide the same level of safety as permanent storage in deep geological formations,[20] due to the necessary maintenance work on interim storage sites.[21] Moreover, interim storage sites are less resistant to interference from third parties[22] and other external factors. Interim storage is therefore not an orderly way of permanently managing radioactive waste.[23]

Interim storage contributes to a certain extent to the fulfilment of the obligation to reduce human and environmental exposure to radioactivity expressed in §6 of the Radiation Protection Ordinance.[24] For this reason, as recently as the early 1980s, interim storage facilities were considered to adequately fulfil the task of ensuring the lowest possible exposure to radiation.[25] Today, however, it is clear that interim storage facilities for radioactive waste are only temporary and that their status over time, as a result of their use, cannot be changed into a final storage facility for radioactive waste. They are not designed to allow radioactive waste to be stored for an indefinite period.

Placing an obligation on those who generated the radioactive waste to manage it by providing for its interim storage implements the constitutional principle of the "polluter pays". There is no possibility that any of the entities responsible for the radioactive waste's production might evade the obligation to take care of its management until it is transferred (in the distant future) to a final disposal facility, as it is subject to the obligation of interim storage.

2. Interim storage of radioactive waste on the premises of nuclear power plants

The obligation to deposit radioactive waste in a central interim storage facility common to all nuclear operators was modified under *Atomausstieg I*. Nuclear power plant operators, who are also the largest producers of radioactive waste, were exempted from this obligation. Under §9a(3), third sentence, of Atomic Law, an offshoot of this exemption was the obligation on these operators to set up interim (individual) radioactive waste disposal facilities on the premises of nuclear power plants (*Standort-Zwischenlager*) – for those radioactive waste generated by the nuclear power plant in question.

Standort-Zwischenlager facilities are intended to store radioactive waste close to where it is generated until it is transferred to a final repository. The idea is to reduce the transport of radioactive waste, first to a common interim storage facility and then to the final disposal facility.[26] The importance of these nuclear installations is also linked to the fact that the date for the transfer of radioactive waste to the final storage facility is still unknown, as this facility has not yet been built. The capacity of interim storages on nuclear sites is therefore defined to correspond to the consumption of nuclear fuel of the nuclear power plant until the last nuclear reactor is shut down. Hence, even a delay in the establishment of a final repository for radioactive waste would not generate a risk that spent fuel could not be stored, for example due to overfilling of the central interim storage facilities.

The interim storage facilities for radioactive waste on the premises of nuclear power plants were established as one component of *Atomausstieg I*. The relevant provisions of Part IV, point 1 of the agreement of 14 June 2000 between the Federal Government and the energy companies contained the following:

> The energy companies will erect interim [radioactive waste] storage facilities as soon as possible on or near the nuclear power plants. They will work together to establish interim storage facilities for radioactive waste at the nuclear power plant sites before the federal, central interim storage facilities are put into operation.[27]

The political arrangements of *Atomausstieg I* also changed the concept of radioactive waste disposal. The previous concept was based on the centralisation of tasks and the introduction of an obligation to transfer radioactive waste to interim storage facilities run by Länder. Ultimately, their waste was to be transferred to a central disposal facility. Its establishment is the task of the Federation in accordance with §9a(1) of Atomic Law. In connection with the new concept introduced by *Atomausstieg I*, a system of decentralised interim storage facilities was created. It consists of both existing interim storage sites operated by the Länder and 12 newly established interim storage sites on nuclear power plant sites.

Interim storage facilities at power plant sites were established to minimise the transport of spent nuclear fuel.[28] However, their construction has led to the establishment of a significant number of new nuclear facilities for interim storage of radioactive waste. Admittedly, they were built on the site of existing nuclear power plants, so it did not involve the creation of more new nuclear installations on new sites. Nevertheless, there arose an accumulation of large quantities of radioactive material at one site. This consisted of nuclear fuel used on an ongoing basis in individual nuclear reactors at a given nuclear power plant and spent fuel stored in interim storage facilities established on the site of the same nuclear power plant. The political consensus in connection with *Atomausstieg I* and *Atomausstieg II* to shut down the last nuclear reactors in 2022 means, in the context of the interim storage facilities at the nuclear power stations, only that the amount of radioactive waste will not increase indefinitely.

Radioactive waste in interim storage facilities erected on the premises of nuclear power stations is stored in so-called wet containers.[29] They have three functions: to ensure that they remain below a critical state, i.e. that no chain reaction (*Unterkritikalität*) occurs on its own; to cool it down; to shield the spent fuel and to protect it from external influences.[30] The licences granted to nuclear power plant operators for the operation of interim storage facilities on nuclear power plant sites require them to maintain a certain volume of wet storage capacity at all times. The capacity is such that all reactors in a given nuclear power plant can be completely emptied of nuclear fuel[31] at any time. This is undoubtedly one of the preventive measures. In addition, the capacity of any interim storage at nuclear power stations is large enough to store all the spent nuclear fuel in the future until the final shutdown of the power station.[32] The interim storage facilities shall also provide for the storage of radioactive waste from the time the nuclear power plant ceases operation until the radioactive waste is transported to a designated final disposal site.[33] The operating licences for these nuclear installations have been granted for 40 years, starting from the time the first container of radioactive waste is stored.[34] The licences were granted for a limited period because of concerns expressed by local residents that interim storage facilities on the site of the nuclear power plants would eventually become the final – and permanent – repositories for the radioactive waste they contain.[35]

The operator of a nuclear power plant could, under §9a(2), sentence 4, of Atomic Law, apply for exemption from the obligation to establish an interim storage facility on the nuclear power plant site. This could be done if he made a binding declaration as to when he would stop generating electricity in a particular nuclear reactor. This was one way of encouraging nuclear reactor operators to conciliate the shut-down of nuclear reactors. An exemption from the administrative obligation to establish an interim storage facility for radioactive waste was obtained in return for a declaration that the nuclear reactor in question would be shut down. The granting of such an exemption entailed certain legal consequences. According to §9a(2) sentence 5 of Atomic Law, the licence to generate electricity in a given nuclear reactor expires on the date indicated in the application. However, the presented solution with obtaining an exemption is currently normatively empty. This is due to the fact that, in connection with *Atomausstieg II*, the law referred to as the 13th Amendment to the Atomic Law of 31 July 2011[36] clearly indicates the operating length of each nuclear reactor and the amount of energy it can still generate (see §1 of 13th Amendment).

The introduction in 2002 of an obligation to set up interim storage facilities on the premises of nuclear power plants shows the practical way in which the "polluter pays" principle has been implemented. In this case, the operators of the nuclear power plants have been made responsible for the temporary storage of nuclear waste (up to 40 years). This involves considerable technical, organisational and logistical effort. Moreover, it is necessary to ensure the safety of these repositories, as well as to finance their creation and to bear their maintenance costs. Hence, a kind of reward for declaring the end of the use of a given nuclear reactor was to be the exemption from the obligation to operate such an interim storage facility for radioactive waste.

This clarification of the functions of interim storage facilities, in view of the duration of the permits, requires – bearing in mind that the first interim storage facility has been in operation since 2002 – that the central disposal facility becomes operational before 2042. It would, however, be desirable for a central disposal facility to be established and operational as soon as possible. There are many risks associated with the operation of interim storage facilities organised on the premises of nuclear power plants. First of all, radioactive waste (interim storage) and nuclear fuel (in an operating nuclear reactor) are accumulated on the same industrial site. The volume of radioactive waste thus accumulated on the site of each nuclear power plant is illustrated in the Table 2.1.

Table 2.1 Interim Radioactive Waste Storage Facilities at Nuclear Power Plants

No.	*Name of storage facility at nuclear power plant*	*Date of issue of the permit pursuant to Section 6 AtomG*	*Weight [t]*	*Number of stations (occupied in 2012[1])*	*Number of stations (occupied in 2018[2])*	*Start of construction*	*Start of use*
1.	SZL[3] Biblis (Biblis Nuclear Power Plant)	22 September 2003	1400	135 (51)	135 (101)	1 March 2004	18 May 2006
2.	SZL Brokdorf (Brokdorf Nuclear Power Plant)	28 November 2003	1000	100 (16)	100 (33)	5 April 2004	5 March 2007
3.	SZL Brunsbüttel (Brunsbüttel Nuclear Power Plant)	28 November 2003	450	80 (9)	80 (20)	7 October 2003	5 February 2006
4.	SZL Grafenrheinfeld (Grafenrheinfeld Nuclear Power Plant)	12 February 2003	800	88 (20)	88 (30)	22 September 2003	27 February 2006
5.	SZL Grohnde (Grohnde Nuclear Power Plant)	20 December 2002	1000	100 (18)	100 (34)	10 November 2003	27 April 2006
6.	SZLGrundremmingen (Grundremmingen Nuclear Power Plant)	19 December 2003	1850	192 (41)	192 (60)	23 August 2004	25 August 2006
7.	SZL Isar (Isar Nuclear Power Plant)	22 September 2003	1500	152 (25)	152 (59)	14 June 2004	12 March 2007
8.	SZL Krümmel (Krümmel Nuclear Power Plant)	19 December 2003	775	80 (19)	80 (41)	23 April 2004	14 November 2006
9.	SZL Lingen (Lingen Nuclear Power Plant)	6 November 2002	1250	125 (32)	125 (47)	18 October 2000	10 December 2002

10. SZL Neckarwestheim (Neckarwestheim Nuclear Power Plant)	22 September 2003	1600	151 (41)	151 (81)	17 November 2003	6 December 2006
11. SZL Philippsburg (Philippsburg Nuclear Power Plant)	19 December 2003	1600	152 (36)	152 (62)	17 May 2004	19 March 2007
12. SZL Unterweser (Unterweser Nuclear Power Plant)	22 September 2003	800	80 (8)	80 (39)	19 January 2004	18 June 2007
Grand total		14025	1435 (316)	1435 (607)		

1 As of the end of 2012.

2 As of the end of 2018.

3 SZL – Standortzwischenlager, interim storage facility for radioactive waste located at a nuclear power plant.

Source: Compiled from: *Übereinkommen über nukleare Sicherheit. Bericht der Bundesrepublik Deutschland für die Achte Überprüfungstagung im März/April 2020*, Bonn 2019; *Übereinkommen über nukleare Sicherheit. Bericht der Bundesrepublik Deutschland für die Sechste Überprüfungstagung im März/April 2014*, Bonn 2013, p. 179.

3. Assessment by the Federal Constitutional Court in Karlsruhe of the constitutionality of interim storage facilities on the premises of nuclear power plants

The Federal Constitutional Court has also dealt with allegations that the concept of interim storage facilities for radioactive waste at nuclear power stations is provisional.[37] The constitutional complaint concerned the interim storage facility for radioactive waste at the Grafenrheinfeld nuclear power station. The subject of the challenge was §9a(2) sentence 3 of Atomic Law. The applicant was the owner of a dwelling house 1.1 km from the nuclear installation in question, where she and her family lived.[38] The applicant complained that the third sentence of §9a(2) of Atomic Law violated the first sentence of Article 2(2) of Basic Law ("Everyone has the right to life and physical integrity") and the first sentence of Article 19(4) of Basic Law ("If a public authority violates someone's rights, that person shall have legal recourse. If no other jurisdiction is justified, the ordinary legal route shall apply"). The applicant complained that the decentralised interim storage system, with the creation of 13[39] new interim storage facilities for radioactive waste on the site of nuclear power stations, does not properly comply with the State's protective duties which, according to the applicant, derive from the first sentence of Article 2(2) of *Grundgesetz*.[40] According to the applicant, the German State has gradually abdicated its responsibility for the disposal of radioactive waste.[41] Moreover, by allowing the State to establish such an interim storage facility on the site of nuclear power stations, the applicant takes the view that the constitutional standard of protection by the State of the health of its citizens against damage by third parties is neither guaranteed nor fulfilled.[42] And since the problem of the lack of a final repository for radioactive waste has not been resolved, this gives rise, according to the applicant, to a risk that the interim storage facility on the site of the nuclear power plant will in time actually become a final repository for radioactive waste.[43] The applicant also complained that the interim storage facility at the Grafenrheinfeld nuclear power station was constructed as a single hall.[44] According to the applicant, no additional measures were adopted to mitigate the various risks to which the installation is exposed.[45] In fact, according to the applicant, the design of the installation increases the risk of radioactive discharges into the environment.[46] A comparative analysis of the technical design of other interim storage facilities built on the site of nuclear power stations reveals that they are similar in design to the structure at issue in these proceedings. In that regard, the arguments put forward by the applicant apply to most interim storage facilities in Germany. In particular, the release of radiation into the environment could occur in the event of an accident or also following deliberate action by third parties, for example a terrorist attack by means of a passenger aircraft.[47]

Having assessed the arguments raised by the applicant, the Federal Constitutional Court decided that the complaint would not be accepted for examination on its merits, as it did not contain any fundamental constitutional issue.[48] In justifying the dismissal of the constitutional complaint, the FCC referred to the concept of Restrisiko, developed on the basis of the so-called Kalkar ruling.[49] According to the Court, in this respect the applicant is obliged to bear the risks associated with the commercial use of nuclear energy.[50] The FCC pointed out that to require a level of protection which excludes with absolute certainty the risk that the fundamental rights of individuals may be infringed by technical installations which require state authorisation to be built and to commence operation would be to go beyond the bounds of human knowledge.[51] That, in turn, would entail an official prohibition on the use of technology.[52] In shaping the social order, however, judgement must be exercised on the basis of practical knowledge (*praktischer Vernunft*) as to what can be done.[53] According to the FCC, the uncertainty arising from the use of practical judgement as the yardstick for evaluation is to be attributed to the limits of human cognition – and thus uncertainty about the limits of human cognition is inevitable.[54] At the same time, citizens have to bear this uncertainty because it is an unavoidable social burden.[55]

The application of this reasoning to the present case means that the FCC has extended the Restrisiko test developed in Kalkar judgment also to interim storage facilities on nuclear sites. The Court pointed out that, in substantive terms, the authorisations are based on a legal basis entirely similar to that on which the Restrisiko test was formulated in Kalkar.[56] The relevance of the Kalkar standard is to uphold its validity and to provide a comprehensive answer by FCC to the case in question.

In the FCC's view, the pleas of unconstitutionality put forward by the applicant are not capable of overcoming the standard developed in the FCC case-law.[57] In so doing, the Court saw no need to revise its findings, well established in its previous case-law, on the risk posed by nuclear installations.[58] In the FCC's view, the disposal of radioactive material in temporary storage facilities on the site of nuclear power stations does not lead to an infringement of the fundamental rights of third parties (individuals)[59] . Nor, therefore, does the applicant have a claim to be able to require the State to establish a system of centralised interim storage facilities in connection with its responsibility for the disposal of radioactive waste.[60] The Court did not share the view that an interim storage site on the site of a nuclear power plant posed a greater risk than a single centralised interim storage facility for radioactive waste.[61] The FCC pointed out that interim storage facilities at nuclear power plants are operated under State supervision.[62] The German public authorities also face similar technical problems when organising an interim storage facility as the energy companies that have set up interim storage facilities at nuclear power plants. Hence, it is not possible to "practically exclude"[63] a violation of fundamental rights, since they are supposed, according to the FCC, to provide a standard of protection similar to state (central) interim storage facilities for radioactive waste.[64] However, such a positioning of the matter by the Court seems to be an oversimplification. The creation of interim storage facilities on the site of nuclear power plants immediately after *Atomausstieg I* means that both the nuclear fuel currently in use in a given reactor and the spent nuclear fuel from that plant will be stored there for the next several years. In addition, interim storage facilities for radioactive waste at power stations are above-ground installations. The interim storage facilities operated by the Länder, on the other hand, are partly underground installations. As such, they may be less vulnerable to threats from deliberate action by third parties (e.g. a terrorist attack). Although the substantive legal prerequisites under Atomic Law may coincide, in reality the installations in question pose different types of risk. The FCC's reliance solely on the wording of Atomic Law entails the risk of classifying a partially different factual situation under the same substantive law category. From a risk assessment perspective, they are also completely different.

The Court also found that the applicant's argument that the chosen concept of interim storage of radioactive waste by the energy companies themselves on the site of nuclear power stations amounts to a waiver by the German State of the possibility of ensuring the best possible level of protection of fundamental rights fails.[65] It does not follow from the first sentence of Article 2(2) of *Grundgesetz* what safeguards are required to ensure that fundamental rights are not infringed in practice.[66] The concept of the "practical exclusion" of the risk of an infringement of fundamental rights should be explained here. According to the FCC, the provisions of Atomic Law (§6(2) items 1–4) on the authorisation of the operation of an interim storage facility for radioactive waste on the site of a nuclear power station require that the dangers and risks associated with the storage of radioactive waste as well as the risks associated with accidents and deliberate interference by third parties be practically excluded.[67] The same interpretation of the provisions in question is also binding on the administrative authorities and the courts.[68] The applicant is not entitled to insist on a higher standard of protection which exceeds the level of risk which she has to bear as a result of the concept of so-called Restrisiko.[69] According to the FCC, the same also applies to the technical aspect of the concept of interim storage facilities for radioactive waste erected on the site of nuclear power stations. If, in the case of a construction of radioactive waste containers authorised by the State, the risk of damage to the goods of third parties is practically excluded, it does not follow from a constitutional perspective that further protective measures should be taken.[70] The decisive factor is whether the protective measures have been developed in accordance with the state of the art.[71] It follows from a well-established case law of the administrative courts[72] under the substantively similar provisions of §7(2) No 3 and No 5 of Atomic Law that it is the executive authorities that are responsible for the identification and assessment of risks.[73] Therefore, the administrative courts, when examining the authorisations granted by the administrative authorities, have a limited margin of discretion as to whether the identification and assessment of risks carried out by the authority in question was based on an adequate body of data.[74] In addition, the administrative courts will also assess whether the State, when granting an authorisation, relies on the current and best state of knowledge and technology at the time when the authorisation was granted.[75] The above-mentioned reasoning from previous case law on other nuclear installations – in addition to interim storage facilities on the site of nuclear power plants – the administrative courts also transfer to administrative decisions on the storage of radioactive material by energy companies in interim storage facilities for radioactive waste erected on the site of nuclear power plants.[76] The Federal Administrative Court has confirmed this approach.[77] The applicant has not succeeded in demonstrating that the scope of administrative review does not satisfy constitutional requirements.[78]

The Court also disagreed with the applicant's argument that the new concept of disposal of radioactive waste, with decentralised interim storage facilities for radioactive waste on the site of nuclear power stations, constituted a departure from the previous system, which was supposed to be characterised by a higher level of safety. Consequently, the level of constitutional protection was allegedly reduced in an unconstitutional manner.[79] The Court pointed out that the increase in the number of interim storage sites should not be regarded as an accumulation of individual risks independently of each other and then presented as a generalised risk (*Kollektivrisiko*) in order to assess the compatibility of the contested provisions with Article 2(2), first sentence, of Basic Law.[80] The Court pointed out that the correct perspective is rather to view the temporary storage of radioactive waste on the site of nuclear power plants as an individual risk of the individual.[81] This individual risk, according to the FCC, does not increase or decrease as a result of the large number of different individual risks.[82]

Similarly, the Court rejected the applicant's argument concerning the risk of exposure to excessive radioactivity due to the failure to take appropriate precautions when constructing an interim storage facility for radioactive waste at the site of the nuclear power station.[83] In the event of adverse weather conditions and the shelling of the interim storage site by small arms, the applicant would have faced an exposure of 112 millisieverts of radioactivity (with an exposure period of seven days).[84] This is a higher level of radioactive exposure than that which the Administrative Court took into account. That court predicted a radiation exposure of 100 millisieverts during the evacuation of the population (ionising radiation exposure period – seven days).[85] However, according to estimates by the Federal Office for Radiation Protection (*Bundesamt für Strahlenschutz*), exceeding this level is in fact excluded.[86] The administrative courts therefore assessed the risk as highly unlikely to occur in the scenario of the most likely serious possible consequences.[87] That was also the reason why the administrative courts did not question the assessment of the possible facts by the administrative authority in question.[88] The FCC considered that the infringement of the applicant's fundamental rights on that ground has not been demonstrated with sufficient clarity.[89]

4. Obligation of the Federation to permanently store radioactive waste

Atomic Law provides for a clear division of tasks between Länder and the federal authorities with regard to radioactive waste. Under the first sentence of §9a(3) of Atomic Law, Länder are obliged to temporarily store all radioactive waste which has been generated within their jurisdiction. The Federation, on the other hand, is obliged to establish a repository(s) for the final storage of radioactive waste (§9a(3), sentence 1). The division of tasks is not even. In the case of Länder, it applies only to those states on whose territory radioactive waste has been (is being or will be) generated. The Federation has been given the most difficult task of developing the concept of a final repository (disposal facility), constructing it and then managing it. This disposal facility will be obliged to accept radioactive waste from the entire territory of the Federal Republic of Germany.

Given the challenge faced by the federal authorities, one can understand the reasons why such a division of tasks between the Federation (disposal facility) and the Länder (provisional interim repositories) was introduced. Furthermore, the distribution of radioactive waste disposal responsibilities among the different levels of government as interrelated tasks can be appreciated as a kind of check and balance mechanism between the different levels of government.[90] This harmonises particularly well with the German political system, in which the authorities in the various Länder often represent a different political camp from the one currently governing the Federation. The political pluralism of the various institutions responsible for carrying out related tasks, thus guaranteed, promotes greater mutual control of the actions taken by the various authorities. This should be viewed positively, especially with regard to such an extremely responsible issue as radioactive waste.

At the same time, the possibility was allowed for Länder or the Federation to use third parties, i.e. private law entities, for these matters (§9a(3) sentence 2). This phenomenon is referred to both in FCC case law and in doctrine as the "privatisation" of disposal of radioactive waste.[91] The doctrine unanimously accepts the admissibility of such a solution only by way of legislation,[92] which means that this formal condition is fulfilled. It should be noted, however, that the legislator followed the recommendations formulated by the commission for the final disposal of radioactive waste and the possibility of outsourcing this public task of operating the disposal facility to a private entity was statutorily excluded.

As regards the potential "privatisation" of radioactive waste management, Atomic Law has adopted two levels of possible organisational and regulatory solutions.[93] The first level would be to entrust a private entity with the performance of certain public tasks (*Beleihungsmodell*).[94] The second level would be the establishment of a legal entity under public law to which the public task of setting up a perpetual storage facility for radioactive waste could be transferred in its entirety.[95] The members of such a newly established legal entity would be those energy companies which are responsible for the generation of radioactive waste.[96]

An even broader scope of recourse to third parties is afforded to the Federation by §9a(3) sentence 3 of Atomic Law. Pursuant to this provision, the Federation may, to the extent necessary, fully or partly, transfer its tasks and the related public-law powers to a third party. The prerequisite is that the third party in question guarantees the lawful fulfilment of the tasks entrusted to it. However, the scope of the obligations transferred to the private entity may also include some of the tasks incumbent on the Federation in this respect. It is emphasised that the transfer of responsibilities does not imply a transfer of responsibility for the task.[97] The construction of a final disposal facility is still a state task.[98] The transfer to a third party of the responsibility for establishing and operating an interim storage facility does not reduce the tasks of the State (Federation), as the Federation is required to supervise the third party in the performance of this task.[99] The assignment of tasks in the form of operation of an interim storage facility to a third party under the third sentence of §9a(3) of the Atomic Law thus differs from the solution provided by the second sentence of §9a(3) by adding to the provision of assistance the assignment of certain state powers.

At the same time, the third party is subject to supervision by the Federation in this respect (§9a(3) sentence 3 *in fine*). One manifestation of the supervision exercised is that appeals against decisions made by the third party are to be heard by the supervisory authority (§9a(3) sentence 9). The third party has been empowered to charge fees to cover the costs of securing and storing radioactive waste (§9a(3) sentence 4). This was done by entrusting the operation of the Gorleben repository to an entity called: *Deutsche Gesellschaft zum Bau und Betrieb von Endlagern für Abfallstoffe mbH.*[100]

The arguments put forward for such a "privatisation" solution allegedly relate largely to the economic side of such a project. First of all, public authorities would not be able to carry out large industrial projects in an economically efficient way.[101] Furthermore, the privatisation of radioactive waste management and disposal by entrusting the operation of the interim storage facility to private entities is expected to bring budget savings for the Federation itself.[102] Entrusting tasks to a third party is also intended to ensure that the tasks entrusted to it are carried out in an economically efficient manner.[103] Efficiency is to be manifested primarily in the area of efficient management.[104]

The arguments against entrusting this task, which is incumbent on the Federation, to private bodies are based firstly on the fact that the alleged savings in staff costs on the Federation's part do not take into account the costs associated with the supervision exercised by the State over this third entity.[105] Another hidden cost item is that the State has to guarantee the physical security of such an interim storage site, even if it is operated by a private entity. Moreover, it is stressed that the State has a duty to ensure the general good, and in this area the State has deprived itself of this task.[106] Nevertheless, the State still has a duty to guarantee the management and disposal of radioactive waste.[107] This also applies in the event of failure of the entity entrusted with this task.

It will take hundreds, if not thousands of years, to control the matters for which the exercise of competence has been entrusted (due to the very long half-life of the isotopes uranium and plutonium).[108] It is important to take into account that many risks can arise during this long time.[109] That is why the state, as the most responsible organisational structure, should have priority in carrying out this task on its own.[110] Another problematic issue is conflict of interest.[111] In the case of the interim storage facility, it should be noted that the company was set up jointly by the energy companies responsible for the production of most of the radioactive waste to be managed. This gives rise to legitimate concerns that the entities responsible for the waste will be too closely linked to the entity entrusted with the task of disposing of the radioactive waste.[112] In connection with the final disposal of radioactive waste, the protection of third parties, the protection of the environment and constant precaution should be paramount.[113] However, entrusting the operation of an interim storage facility to a private entity that would carry out this public task on the basis of economic and financial criteria could be done with due care.[114] Some authors therefore advocate the complete separation of the performance of the Federation's tasks in the area of the final disposal of radioactive waste from those responsible for its generation, who would like to perform this task as cheaply as possible.[115]

While the criticism is valid in terms of not allowing responsibility to be taken away from the State for carrying out tasks relating to the interim storage and permanent disposal of radioactive waste, it would seem that this activity itself could be undertaken by a third party – at least in regards to interim storage. It would be important in this case to ensure strict supervision of these activities. Moreover, the cost of state supervision should be covered by fees paid by the obliged entities.

5. Regulatory framework of the liability of the Federation for the infringement of professional duties by a third party that was entrusted by the Federation with executing public tasks

Since the possibility of a private entity managing a radioactive waste repository has been considered, attention should be paid to the way in which the liability of the State for any damage caused by such a third party is regulated. This is important in view of the huge quantities of radioactive waste entrusted to that entity, the safe management of which is one of the most important public tasks. Under Atomic Law, this issue has been resolved in an interesting way. According to the provision of Article 9a(3) sentence 6, the Federation shall not be liable for the breach of official duties by a third party. To cover damages resulting from a breach of duty, the third party is obliged to provide security against possible damage (*Schadensvorsorge*). The amount of such security must be sufficient to cover possible damage. Insuring such a risk is one example of providing this security.[116] Importantly, the provisions of Article 9a of Atomic Law do not affect the general principles of liability regulated in Article 25 of Atomic Law. If the insurance provided does not manage to cover the damages, the direct liability will be borne by the operator of the nuclear installation, although only up to the amount of €2.5 billion.[117] Insofar as the Federation has entrusted third parties with the performance of public tasks, exemption from liability for damages pursuant to Article 25 may be granted only up to the amount of €2.5 billion (Article 9a subsection 3, sentence 8). Above this amount, the Federation will always be liable. It should be noted here that such a solution has only been possible since 2011 – previously, pursuant to Article 36 of Atomic Law, the Federation was jointly and severally liable for 75%. The rest of the liability fell on the state in which the nuclear installation in question was located or on the state that had licensed the nuclear installation to which the damage occurred.

This means that entrusting a third party with the fulfilment of statutory obligations does not absolve the public authorities of their responsibility for the disposal of radioactive waste. In the absence of such a provision, the general principle would be that the legal person entrusted with a particular public task bears sole responsibility.[118]

In addition, the federal legislature took seriously the risk that the basic cover for nuclear damage (*Schadensvorsorge*) would not be sufficient.[119] This could occur for various reasons. This is evidenced by the two additional recourse claims introduced into Atomic Law in the provisions of Article 37(1)(3) and Article 46(1)(3).[120] The first case is the possibility of a recourse claim against the operator of a nuclear installation if the security proves to be insufficient as regards the extent of the damage to be covered or its amount in relation to the officially imposed requirements. The second case concerns penalty provisions. A fine is to be imposed on a person who has intentionally or unintentionally acted against ensuring security by the nuclear installation operator at an officially designated level.

There is no doubt that only the State, i.e. the Federation, is the entity that can assume liability for compensation without an upper limit. The central role played by the State is best illustrated by the example of the Japanese energy company TEPCO, operator of the Fukushima nuclear power plant. The extent of the damage and the number of measures which had to be taken in connection with the nuclear reactor disaster, as well as the enormous costs that had to be borne in connection with both the continuous clean-up of the disaster and the compensation payments, clearly show the role of the state in such a situation. This role cannot be privatised or eliminated. Nuclear energy at every stage involves an extremely important role and participation of the state, even when the investors are private energy companies, and some of the public tasks in this area will be transferred to private entities.

In the case of damage which may occur in connection with the storage of radioactive waste, it is not possible to set an upper limit for such liability. Likewise, it is not possible to set an upper limit on the amount of cover for commercial insurance. Those who suffer nuclear damage will consequently be exposed to the credit risk of the insured entity and the policyholders. This means that the ability to settle their claims will be linked to the solvency of both the entity responsible for the damage and the insurance (or reinsurance) company. For this reason, the exclusion of the Federation's liability provided by Article 9a(3) sentence 8 of Atomic Law is only partial. Another reason is also given for the fact that liability rests with the Federation. The State, by granting a licence to operate a nuclear installation (as well as all other nuclear installations), bears joint responsibility for this activity, to which the risk of accidents and damage is inherent.[121]

The solution adopted in form of introducing unlimited liability for the Federation (once nuclear damage exceeds the level of €2.5 billion) is also significantly cheaper for the nuclear industry, as the premiums are lower in the end. This is because there is no need to obtain the highest possible insured sum (e.g. at the level of €250 billion), as the Federation will always be liable above a certain level (here: €2.5 billion). At the same time, the Federation is the most solvent entity. This is evidenced, on one hand, by the highest creditworthiness awarded to German federal debt securities by the international capital markets. This excellent assessment of the solvency of the German state is followed by the very low risk premium demanded by capital market participants – it even started to turn negative in July 2016. On the other hand, the tax jurisdiction of the German state covers more than 80 million individuals and countless other private and public law entities, giving the opportunity to tax them additionally should the need arise.

The Federation may obtain the additional funding it needs at any given time by introducing (or increasing) taxes or other public levies. Introducing the Federation as the last entity to bear liability for compensation is the right solution, as it gives the injured parties a guarantee that their claims will be settled. The level at which the Federation will be liable must not be too low. Otherwise, this will mean that the state will be heavily subsidising the nuclear industry by reducing its compulsory insurance contributions.

6. Securing funding from radioactive waste generators for the costs of radioactive waste management and disposal

Just as important as determining how to manage radioactive waste is determining how to secure funding for the management and future disposal of radioactive waste.

On the organisational and financial side, several solutions are possible to secure funding from those who bear the cost of the disposal selection process, i.e. the radioactive waste generators. In the literature, discussions have revolved around three approaches that are applicable to responsible energy companies. The first is for these companies to set aside accounting specific reserves. The second is to create a voluntary foundation that would assume all the responsibilities for managing radioactive waste. The third is the collection of forced fees for the state's special purpose fund.

The first solution is for energy companies to set aside specific reserves to pay for the dismantling and decontamination of nuclear power plants and the cost of final disposal of radioactive waste. To date, setting aside specific reserves has been widely used by energy companies as a way to prepare for these costs in the future. It is a solution rooted primarily in accounting and corporate law. It needs to be discussed in detail in order to shed light on its possible consequences and to understand the arguments raised against it, e.g. concerning a possible breach of the constitutional principle of "the polluter pays".[122]

Establishing a specific reserve means that liabilities for a specific purpose are booked on the liabilities side of the company's balance sheet.[123] The costs of dismantling nuclear power plants and decontaminating them, and the costs of final disposal of radioactive waste (i.e. the cost of holding radioactive waste in interim storage facilities and then in a final disposal facility) may be just such a purpose. Setting aside a reserve will reduce the company's profit in the year in which the reserve is established.[124] The funds used to establish the reserve will not be taxable, nor can they be distributed as dividends.[125]

Reserves are engaged as follows. When a nuclear power plant is decommissioned and is designated for decontamination, the reserve set aside for this purpose is released.[126] The costs of dismantling and shutting down are then drawn from the assets of that energy company.[127] If the expenditure to be incurred corresponds to the amount of the established reserve, there will be no charge to the company's profit[128] (in a given quarter and financial year). There will be a simultaneous reduction of the balance sheet totals in the amount corresponding to the released specific reserve (on the liabilities side) and used revenues (on the assets side).[129] On the other hand, it is important to distinguish between specific reserves and supplementary capital created for some purpose. The latter is based on the company's own already accumulated capital, while the specific reserves created are based on foreign capital yet to come into the company. This is because specific reserves are a way of using future profit. The fundamental factor is not just the amount of the specific reserves.[130] The decisive factor will be whether the company and its underlying assets have the potential to generate sufficient cash flow in the future to enable them to be utilised on the asset side of the company's balance sheet.[131] Specific reserves are based primarily on the assumption that a company must survive until a particular specific reserve is needed. Thus, a given business entity cannot go bankrupt, which is due to the lack of specific protection for the established reserves within the bankruptcy proceedings.[132] It is therefore problematic that, although the specific reserves are created for a specific public purpose (decontamination of nuclear plants and disposal of radioactive waste), under this scenario the state would have no legally protected claim on the specific reserves.[133] As far as these specific reserves are concerned, only the respective energy company will be obliged to make certain dispositions. The condition, however, is that there must still be assets left in the bankruptcy estate to make this possible. Then, however, specific reserves will not be a priority in satisfaction against the bankruptcy estate.[134] Considering the financial stability and possible bankruptcy of an energy company is important because the financial performance of these companies has deteriorated significantly. This has been noted since Germany began its energy revolution *(Energiewende)* of abandoning the use of fossil fuels to meet its energy needs and switching to energy from renewable sources.

If the energy company responsible for generating the radioactive waste does not go bankrupt and makes it to the time of payment, the company must still have adequate assets. Another important element to enable the scenario in question is that the entity in question must be generating sufficiently high revenues at the time. For energy companies, it is difficult to estimate the likely amount and certainty of future revenues.[135] This can be done by the method of estimating the possible revenues of the different parts of the company, in this case – the individual power plants.[136] In the event of inadequate (i.e. insufficient) revenues, the specific reserve will be realised by drawing on the profit for the year. If this, too, proves insufficient, one will need to draw on the company's capital and, secondarily, its fixed assets. The last resort will be the possible liquidation of the company and the use of share capital.

Sureties and guarantees provided by the parent company and the contract governing the transfer of profits to the parent company may be a way to prevent such a development, i.e. lack of funds due to the entity's bankruptcy or insufficient assets in the company.[137] It is indicated that such safeguards have been established only until 2022.[138] In addition, they can be terminated at any time.[139] It is also important to note that the collateral will not represent much value in the event of the collapse of the energy company.

The method of hedging the cost of radioactive waste disposal described here has been widely used by energy companies. The reserves thus set aside at the end of 2013 amounted to about 36 billion euros[140] and, according to estimates for 2014, to about 38 billion euros.[141] The amount of reserves may have been why, until recently, the Federal Government considered it a proven system for securing funding for the costs of radioactive waste management.[142] Specific reserves were established not only to cover the cost of radioactive waste disposal, but also to perform three tasks: shut down the nuclear power plant, decontaminate and dismantle it, and dispose the radioactive waste (including the cost of radioactive waste disposal). When one considers that the costs of decommissioning, decontamination and subsequent dismantling of a nuclear power plant cannot be precisely determined in advance, but only after that work has been completed, it is difficult to predict whether any of the specific reserves would still be available for the management, neutralisation and disposal of radioactive waste.

Doubts about the effectiveness of this method have begun to emerge in the literature.[143] The reason was that from a certain point on there was a radical change in the strategy of energy companies responsible for the generation of radioactive waste, and the corporate transformations that were taking place as a result. The public debate was sparked by E.ON's decision to split into two separate companies (in effect, two separate capital groups): Uniper and E.ON.[144] Uniper acquired the infrastructure of the conventional power industry (including nuclear power plants). In turn, E.ON acquired business lines based on the generation of electricity from renewable energy sources and the distribution of energy to end customers.

In view of such developments concerning corporate changes in the energy companies that are responsible for the generation of radioactive waste, the topic of other possible ways to provide funds for the management of radioactive waste, alternative to the establishment of specific reserves, has emerged in the public debate. The next two solutions are to create a voluntary foundation or to impose forced fees for the state's special purpose fund.

The concept of creating a foundation was most likely based on the model that was used in the Ruhr region. It was based on the concept that the sorting out of stranded costs after a period of hard coal mining in Germany would also enable the termination of coal mining. In 2007, the RAG-Stiftung Foundation was established which from 2019 assumed the following costs: polder maintenance, mine water management and groundwater treatment.[145] These costs are referred to as perpetual (*Ewigkeitslasten, Erblasten* or *Ewigkeitskosten*), as the cessation of these activities would lead to the Ruhr region being completely submerged.[146] The purpose of this foundation is to avoid public financing of these tasks which represent stranded costs from mining activities in the area.[147] There is a clear parallel here to the problems that have arisen in the wake of nuclear power. The RAG-Stiftung Foundation was established as a result of an agreement between the Federal Government, the state governments of Rhineland-Westphalia and Saarland and the mining companies RAG AG (mining) and IG BCE (mining machinery).[148] The solution is that the public authorities, together with the mining companies, agreed on how the companies would carry out further work on mining damage caused by coal mining. This is even clearer with regard to the shareholders of RAG joint stock company – these include E.ON, RWE, ThyssenKrup and Societe Nouvelle Sidechar.[149] The shares of the individual shareholders in RAG were donated to the RAG-Stiftung Foundation for the symbolic sum of 1 euro.[150] Simultaneous transfers of assets to this foundation were conducted.[151] By 2018, the accumulation of assets of the RAG-Stiftung Foundation was completed.[152] The income from the accumulated assets is to be used to fund the perpetual costs to prevent the area from being submerged by mining activities.[153] As of the end of 2011, RAG-Stiftung had a balance sheet total of approximately 14.2 billion euros,[154] and revenues of 3.1 billion euros.[155] In contrast, at the end of 2016, total assets on the asset side amounted to 20.7 billion euros,[156] and revenue amounted to 1.75 billion euros.[157]

The literature indicates that self-financing by the RAG-Stiftung Foundation is an uncertain goal.[158] If the foundation were to run out of funds to finance "perpetual costs", the individual states would then cover part of the shortfall (for mines from their territory), with the Federation making up one-third of the missing funds.[159] Furthermore, the RAG-Stiftung Foundation has always maintained that the tasks resulting from "perpetual costs" do not include typical mining damages that are a nuisance to local residents.[160] This results in a significant break in the protection provided to those affected by mining damage. Here, too, the state will most likely bear shared responsibility, since the mining company was transferred to the RAG Foundation. This solution means that relieving the companies that are shareholders in RAG joint stock company from paying "perpetual costs" was undoubtedly a success. However, the companies had to pay a price – they donated assets to the foundation. However, it remains to be seen whether the RAG Foundation's primary goal of cost avoidance by the state will be achieved at all. Thus, the risk is no longer borne by the companies, but has become a matter for the federal states and the Federation should costs rise.

The creation of a similar foundation for the nuclear power industry, described as a voluntary act, may be a solution to the problem of bearing the costs of radioactive waste disposal.[161] The term "voluntary act" probably has to do with the fact that the solutions for creating foundations are based on civil law standards, and state coercion is absent in them. However, it is hard to imagine that such an agreement would not include public authorities and that it would not include all energy companies. Otherwise, this agreement would be ineffective and lead to a kind of dualism in the approach to determining how to finance the costs of decontaminating nuclear plants, as well as neutralising and disposing of radioactive waste.

The model for a foundation-based solution that has been considered in the public debate would be the voluntary transfer of nuclear power plants and their specific reserves to a foundation or a special purpose vehicle.[162] It should be emphasised here that it is not possible to transfer to such a foundation the legal title to established specific reserves.[163] The RAG-Stiftung Foundation would be a model for this.[164] The basic problem with this solution is that transferring nuclear power plant operators, i.e. companies with established specific reserves, to a new foundation (or a special purpose vehicle) will not become a stable source of revenue at all. According to *Atomausstieg II*, by 2022 at the latest, all nuclear reactors in Germany are expected to cease operation. This means that, henceforth, nuclear plant operators will no longer have revenue from receipts for electricity generated. The source from which to create specific reserves will be depleted.[165] At the same time, most of the assets of nuclear power plant operators are likely to be worthless, so they will no longer serve in any economic activity.

Even the contribution of other conventional power plants to the assets of such a specific purpose foundation will not be adequate to provide funding for the costs of radioactive waste disposal. First, it is questionable whether conventional power plants in the German energy market will be a reliable source of revenue or will cause losses. Second, the cost structure for decontaminating nuclear power plants and neutralising radioactive waste will be quite different from the "perpetual cost" structure of the RAG-Stiftung Foundation. Implementing the Federation's current plans for neutralising radioactive waste will impose significant costs over the next several decades. These costs will include decontaminating and dismantling all nuclear power plants, preparing radioactive waste for disposal, funding the selection of a suitable site for a radioactive waste disposal facility, and then erecting the final disposal facility.[166] After a certain point, all that will be left is the cost of overseeing the radioactive waste disposal facility for a million years after it is finally sealed,[167] and the ongoing cost of maintaining the final disposal facility. The cost structure to be borne is therefore different from that of the RAG-Stiftung Foundation. If the two structures were similar, funding could be provided from the resources of the specific reserve scheme once the appropriate assets were contributed. However, in the case presented here, this would most likely mean that the foundation would have to liquidate most of its assets. The level of current revenues from the assets would not be sufficient to cover the costs which will be significant for several decades and will only decrease later to reach a constant, predictable level.

In addition, a solution based on the foundation model raises questions about its constitutionality. The establishment of a foundation should be qualified as a kind of instrument of informal action by public authorities.[168] In the area of nuclear power, this was criticised with the implementation of *Atomausstieg I*,[169] and later the so-called *Laufzeitverlängerung*.[170] In this case, however, it is intended to be the kind of informal and consensual state action that would avoid statutory intervention. And this is why such a model is not criticised in the literature.[171] At the same time, the foundation scenario would have to be classified as just such a case because it would exacerbate the need for nuclear power plant operators to carry out their responsibilities for neutralisation and disposal of radioactive waste.[172] It should be noted, however, that if, as a result of the efforts of many actors, a particular action is taken voluntarily to tighten the standard of protection, it is no longer voluntary and is in the nature of state coercion. It is pointed out that such state action would even have the character of nationalisation of enterprises.[173] As one can see, informal and consensual state actions cannot be underestimated.

Moreover, the assessment of the constitutionality of the foundation model notes that entities that have generated radioactive waste are required by Atomic Law to dispose that radioactive waste (§9a) and to bear its costs (§§21a and 21b). So, obligations of a public law nature are imposed on these entities.[174] Given the magnitude of the costs, it is essential that the state prepares such a scheme of funding by responsible parties that ensures an adequate, sufficient volume of funding.[175] The obligation of the state to provide such a financing mechanism stems from the principle of public finance discipline, and in particular from: Article 2, paragraph 2 of *Grundgesetz*, i.e. protection of health and life of the inhabitants, Article 14, paragraph 1 of *Grundgesetz*, i.e. protection of property, and Article 20a of *Grundgesetz*, i.e. the principle of environmental protection.[176] Budgetary discipline must be stressed here, because if the financial scheme developed proves insufficient, then the costs will fall on the Federation and the federal states where the nuclear systems are located. Likewise, the potential failure of due diligence resulting in contamination will result in significant costs to the state in terms of its obligation to provide health care and remediation of environmental damage. Thus, it is in the well-understood interest of the public authorities (federal and individual states) to provide funding that takes into account the time horizon of the obligations arising from the radioactive waste disposal. This will be a perspective that extends beyond the lifetime of the current generation and several generations to come. Thus, it seems reasonable to believe that the presented foundation model will not correspond to the public law obligations of radioactive waste generators.[177] Admittedly, on the basis of Article 20a of *Grundgesetz*, the federal legislature has sufficiently broad discretionary power to recognise possible actions that the establishment of foundations will also be included.[178] However, this position does not take into account the financial aspects presented here. It seems, therefore, that the foundation model does not make it possible to fully carry out the obligations imposed on energy companies, arising from “the polluter pays” principle.

Another solution could be the creation of a state special-purpose fund, to be fed by compulsory payments from nuclear power plant operators.[179] However, the institutional aspect of such a fund is uncertain. This fund could, for example, be based on voluntary contributions from nuclear power plant operators. Voluntary contributions, however, would not guarantee the effectiveness of the fund and the certainty that the purpose for which it was established would be achieved.[180] In the same way, specific reserves established in companies cannot be transferred to the state fund, as their legal and economic structure does not permit this.[181]

In addition to a possible model for such a specific fund, other solutions have been considered in the literature. First, statutory exclusions from the assets of individual nuclear power plant operators were considered as "internal funds" (*interner Fonds*), which could take the form of a forced creation of a supplementary capital by the respective company.[182] Such a solution, which is judged to be relatively benign for businesses, would, however, require considerable bureaucratic activity, with further costs associated with it.[183]

Another solution would be to make changes to the bankruptcy regulations. This would be done by removing from the estate, in the event of the insolvency of the entity in question, a certain amount of funds necessary to meet the financial requirements for the management and neutralisation of radioactive waste.[184] Even if the Federation were granted such statutory priority in the settlement of the claim over the bankruptcy estate of a company, this would not guarantee that a sufficient pool of funds would still remain in the bankruptcy estate to satisfy the claim.[185]

Still another possibility would be to continue to use the parent company's surety structure within the capital group.[186] This solution, however, would still be characterised by uncertainty due to the possibility of termination of such the contract, as well as the possible bankruptcy of the parent company, which would make it impossible to obtain any funds.[187] The idea of shaping a scheme to provide funding for neutralisation of radioactive waste similar to the EU CO2 Emissions Trading Scheme[188] has also been considered. This concept would make it mandatory for the responsible energy companies to redeem waste certificates *(Entsorgrungszertifikaten)*, and the certificates themselves would be auctioned.[189]

Another possible solution would be to create a forced association whose purpose would be to fund the disposal of radioactive waste.[190] The drawback of such a solution, however, would be that it would interfere with the freedom of association guaranteed by Article 9(1) of *Grundgesetz*.[191]

Of the alternatives to a forced fund presented, the voluntary foundation model is indicated in the literature as equally suitable.[192] Whether it is possible to qualify it as a softer measure depends on the final design of the fund regulations.[193]

Such a new public tribute in the form of payments by obligated companies to implement a radioactive waste disposal and management would not serve the state's overall financial needs. Therefore, as a non-tax levy, it would be subject to the assessment of their constitutional permissibility developed by the Federal Constitutional Court.[194] It would probably be pointed out that there could be a kind of collective responsibility in the event of such a joint charge, since individual nuclear power plant operators would be treated as a group and charged.[195] It is unclear whether such a fee would be calculated based on the amount of radioactive waste generated by a given power company. Federal Constitutional Court's jurisprudence is inconsistent here,[196] so a fund shaped this way could be challenged. In terms of the constitutionality of the task in question and the length of time it is funded by the fund, i.e., until the radioactive waste disposal facility is sealed, and then the fees associated with the fixed costs of maintaining the facility are collected, it is important that the federal legislature make a special effort to exercise its oversight responsibilities.[197]

The considerations in the literature presented here need to be supplemented by the effects of the actions of public authorities. At the end of 2015, these took the form of a bill on liability – which continues after a company ceases to exist – for the decommissioning of nuclear power plants and the disposal of radioactive waste (*Entwurf eines Gesetz zur Nachhaftung für Rückbau- und Entsorgungskosten im Kernenergiebereich*).[198] The Federal Government's bill was referred to the Bundestag on 9 November of that year. The justification aptly recognises the paradox of funding a radioactive waste disposal facility. In 2022, revenues from operating nuclear power plants will cease, but the costs of shutting down and decommissioning nuclear power plants and neutralising radioactive waste along with its disposal will not occur until after 2022.[199] This means that these costs will not be able to be financed from the current revenues of nuclear power plant operators. Over the next decades, the source of their funding will be the assets of the operators.[200] A radioactive waste disposal facility is estimated to be available in 2050 at the earliest.[201] Considering that these entities' revenues will end after 2022, concerns about their financial health are justified. The purpose of the bill is to provide funding for the costs of nuclear power plant shutdown and decommissioning and neutralisation of radioactive waste along with its disposal, and to reduce the risk that these costs will be publicly funded.[202]

According to the provision of §1(1) of the bill, the solutions provided by this law are to cover all present and future public liabilities of the operators of nuclear power plants in Germany. This applies only to commercial nuclear reactors (and not to research reactors). These obligations are to include the cost of shutting down and decommissioning the plant in question (§7(3) of Atomic Law), the cost of neutralising radioactive waste (§9a(1)), obligations under §§21a and 21b of Atomic Law and the costs of radioactive waste disposal as defined in the Ordinance and in Chapter 4 of the Standortauswahlgesetz. The bill provided that if a nuclear plant operator failed to make a payment due, the parent company would be liable. Under §1(2) of the bill, if the authority must take substitute action for the nuclear power plant operator during the administrative enforcement phase, then the cost of such substitute action may also be charged to the parent company. Examples of such activities include the interim storage of radioactive waste or its transport.[203] Under the bill, a "parent entity" is to be an entity that directly or indirectly owns at least half of the shares in the company-operator of a nuclear power plant or has at least half of the votes at the general meeting of shareholders or, in specific cases, can decisively influence the entity. The most far-reaching provision of the bill is arguably §1(3) which states that if it is not possible to collect designated public tributes due to the liquidation of the nuclear power plant operator company, a recourse claim against the parent company is possible. At the same time, the scope of this claim is determined in such a way that it is determined to the extent to which the liquidated nuclear power plant operator company would have been liable had it existed. Thus, this means creating a legal fiction of the existence of the entity in question in order to assess the amount of public tribute to be charged to its former parent owner. At the same time, according to §1(3) sentence 2 of the bill, if an administrative authority is required to substitute the actions required by the Atomic Law for the decommissioned nuclear power plant operator, the cost of such action by the administrative authority may also be charged to the parent company. However, it is questionable whether these regulatory changes will also cover conversions of companies (E.ON, RWE and Vattenfall) made even before the bill may come into force. The wording of the bill's provisions, on the other hand, makes it clear that the intent is for it to cover those entities as well.

§3(1) of the bill provided that the liability of a parent entity does not cease by virtue of the fact that the entity ceased to be a parent entity after the effective date of this bill. This will happen through appropriate restructuring within a capital group, which will reduce or prevent the financial liability of the companies. Another scenario would be the sale of the nuclear power plant operator company.[204] This provision should be understood in terms of the purpose of the Act – to prevent the avoidance of financial liability associated with radioactive waste.

At the same time, §3(2) provides that the transfer of the parent's liability to a third party is legally ineffective. The Act contains a time limitation on the liability of entities understood as parent entities under the Act. According to §4, the liability of the parent entity ends when the high-level radioactive waste of the nuclear power plant operator is transferred to the final disposal facility and officially sealed. The timing of these activities is dependent on the availability of the final disposal facility, which project proponents estimated will not occur until 2050 at the earliest.[205] And since adjusting radioactive waste to disposal and its storage will also be needed, the planners suggest adding several decades to the deadline for the sealing of the final disposal facility.[206]

The draft of *Rückbau- und EntsorgungskostennachhaftungsG* presented here addresses concerns about the current legal status raised both in the public debate and in the legal literature. The drafters correctly assessed that the fulfilment of radioactive waste obligations is solely dependent on the future financial status of the nuclear plant operator.[207] Finally, content of the presented bill was included in Article 8 of the Act of 27 January 2017 on regulating anew liability for radioactive waste disposal[208] (*Gesetz zur Neuordnung der Verantwortung in der kerntechnischen Entsorgung*). Implementing by the legislator in the Act of 27 January 2017 the analysed solution will ensure financing of radioactive waste disposal also in the case of bankruptcy of one of the entities responsible for generating radioactive waste.

In order to be able to evaluate the legal solutions, it is also necessary to consider here the context of existing capital ties of individual nuclear power plant operator companies. When one considers the shareholding structure of individual companies, it is striking that the solutions presented in the bill protect minority shareholders. The shareholder structure of the various commercial nuclear reactors currently in operation[209] is diversified. An analysis of the shareholder structure identifies the following minority shareholders: Vattenfall (for the Brunsbüttel nuclear reactor), EON (Emsland, Grundremmingen B and Grundremmingen C), Stadtwerke Bielefeld (Grohnde) and Stadtwerke München (Isar 2). The shape of the Act's arrangements as so presented thus provides that statutory recourse to radioactive waste from these nuclear reactors will not be available to minority shareholders. It should be pointed out that Vattenfall and E.ON will be classified as the parent company in many other nuclear power plants. In contrast, Stadtwerke Bielefeld and Stadtwerke München, which are energy companies owned by the cities of Bielefeld and Munich, will be exempted from the regulation. It seems that this regulation was created in such a way that it could gain the support of all the states of the German federation.

The solution presented in the Act of 27 January 2017 is a break with the fundamental principle of corporate law that shareholders of joint-stock companies are liable only up to the amount of invested capital. The basic economic sense of a commercial company is that there is no shortage of recourse directly against shareholders, even if the company goes bankrupt. In such a case, the shareholder risks rendering their shares in the company worthless. This applies to both private and public law claims. There are judicial attempts to expand liability for the actions of the company beyond itself under the so-called *piercing the corporate veil*[210] concept. But they apply to exceptional situations, their nature is generally limited to torts, and they are not introduced by such explicit legislative intervention. The shape of the proposed solution, while it breaks this rule, does so unevenly since it excludes minority shareholders from the rule. This unequal treatment is not adequately justified. Both the majority shareholder and the minority shareholder made appropriate expenditures for the company they formed and then collected profit from it corresponding to the amount of their shares. Meanwhile, the Act provides for only one group of entities to be charged. A possible justification would be to protect these minority shareholders (the majority shareholders are states or other public authorities, especially at the local government level). The municipal power companies of Stadtwerke Bielefeld and Stadtwerke München will be just such an example. Holding such entities accountable instead of nuclear power plant operators would not be consistent with the purposes of the Act, as public funds could be involved at the end. However, if the legislator made such a distinction between the status of minority shareholders and that of the parent entity precisely for this reason, it should have been explicitly indicated in the text of the bill and in its explanatory memorandum. Whether the drafters were determined to save the finances of the federal states and individual local governments seems doubtful, since the co-owners of the RWE AG are municipal shareholders (cities, municipalities and counties) who hold about 25% of the shares.

It should further be noted that the scope of the Act did not include research reactors. Ten research reactors are currently operating,[211] eight more have been shut down[212] and are awaiting dismantling, and 25 have already been decommissioned.[213] They were operated largely by universities, colleges or research institutes, so this is another group of entities that were not covered by this regulation. It is worth noting that the amount of high-level radioactive waste generated by research reactors is several orders of magnitude lower.

Compared to the various possible solutions considered in the literature, the Federal Government's legislative solution goes the furthest. No entity will ever free itself from liability associated with radioactive waste. This is confirmed, for example, by the accepted legal fiction that the parent company takes over part of the expenses of the now defunct nuclear power plant operator. As long as there is a parent company, it will be possible to require the parent company to pay the costs of the now defunct nuclear power plant operator company. Another argument is that the completion of a high-level radioactive waste final disposal facility and its subsequent sealing is included in the scope of this law.

Enaction of the Act of 27 January 2017 means that its goal of reducing the risk of spending public funds on radioactive waste remains contingent on the financial health of the parent entities. It may therefore turn out that the bankruptcy of energy companies will affect not only the country's energy security, but also the state of public finances. In this case, there may be a recognition (as in the case of systemically important financial institutions) that these companies are too large to fail because of the consequences for the financial sector and the economy. However, it may also be the case that the cost burden of radioactive waste is so great that it leads to the permanent insolvency of an energy company. As a result, its operations will be blocked, jeopardising energy security, for example, due to its significant generation capacity or the provision of distribution services to energy end users. In addition, it will burden public finances because of the need to absorb the costs incurred in disposal of radioactive waste. It is such a combination of circumstances that only the state's rescue of the energy company in question is an option. Security of electricity supply cannot be compromised because of the associated consequences. At the same time, the possible removal of "healthy" assets (e.g. generating units in the renewables sector or the distribution segment) from the bankruptcy estate of an energy company will most likely maintain security of energy supply, although this will inevitably involve the public budget assuming the costs of financing the disposal of radioactive waste. In all likelihood, this would be a no-win situation, so in order to mitigate the consequences of a potential collapse of one of the responsible energy companies, one would rather expect the Federal Government to carry out an appropriate rescue and aid programme.

Notes

1 Bundesminister des Innern, *Antwort der Bundesregierung auf die Große Anfrage der Abgeordneten Dr. Laufs, Dr. Dregger, Spranger, Dr. Riesenhuber, Dr. Miltner, Lenzer, Broll, Fellner, Dr. von Geldern, Gerlach, Dr. Waffenschmidt, Dr. Bugl, Gerstein, Frau Hürland, Kolb, Dr. George, Dr. Jobst, Dr. Köhler (Wolfsburg), Dr. Kunz (Weiden), Magin, Pfeffermann, Prangenberg, Schwarz, Dr. Stavenhagen und der Fraktion der CDU/CSU – Drucksache 9/858 – Verantwortung des Bundes für Sicherstellung und Endlagerung radioaktiver Abfälle in der Bundesrepublik Deutschland* of 22 December 1981, „Deutscher Bundestag Drucksache 9/1231", p. 3.

2 J.Olliges, *A »deliberative turn« in German nuclear waste governance?* [in:] A.Brunnengräber, M.Di Nucci (eds.), *Conflicts, participation and acceptability in nuclear waste governance*, Wiesbaden 2019, p. 262; A.Brunnengräber, *The wicked problem of long term radioactive waste governance* [in:] A.Brunnengräber, M.Di Nucci (eds.), *Conflicts, participation and acceptability in nuclear waste governance*, Wiesbaden 2019, p. 338; C.Drögemüller, *Schlüsselakteure der Endlager-Governance. Entsorgungsoptionen und – strategien radioaktiver Abfälle aus Sicht regionaler Akteure*, Wiesbaden 2018, p. 2; J.Kuhbier, U.Prall, *Errichtung und Betrieb von Endlagern für radioaktive Abfälle durch Beliehene?*, „ZUR" 2009, vol. 7–8, p. 359.

3 M.Ramana, *Why technical solutions are insufficient. The abiding conundrum of nuclear waste* [in:] A.Brunnengräber, M.Di Nucci (eds.), *Conflicts . . .*, p. 27; O.Däuper, A.Bernstorff, *Gesetz zur Suche und Auswahl eines Standortes für die Endlagerung radioaktiver Abfälle – zugleich ein Vorschlag für die Agenda der „Kommission Lagerung hoch radioaktiver Abfallstoffe"*, „ZUR" 2014, p. 24; B.Bonin, *Jak postępować z odpadami jądrowymi?* [in:] K.Jeleń, Z.Rau (eds.), *Energetyka jądrowa w Polsce*, Warsaw 2012, p. 684. For example, the launch of such a perpetual radioactive waste repository in France is planned for 2025; see B.Bonin, p. 685.

4 Bundesminister des Innern, *Antwort* . . . , p. 1.
5 So in: H.Haedrich, *Zur Zulässigkeit der Wiederaufarbeitung abgebrannter Brennelemente aus deutschen Kernkraftwerken in anderen EG-Mitgliedstaaten* "NVwZ" 1993, p. 1038.
6 Bundesminister des Innern, *Antwort* . . . , p. 1.
7 M.Vogt, *Zur ethischen Bewertung der Atomenergie nach Tschernobyl und Fukushima* [in:] J.Ostheimer, M.Vogt (eds.), *Die Moral der Energiewende. Risikowahrnehmung im Wandel m Beispiel der Atomenergie*, Stuttgart 2014, p. 24.
8 U.Wollenteit, *Gorleben und kein Ende*, "ZUR" 2014, p. 324.
9 Bundesminister des Innern, *Antwort* . . . , p. 1. See also W.Alley, R.Alley, *Too hot to touch. The problem of high-level nuclear waste*, Cambridge 2012, pp. 29–41.
10 C.Offermann, *Die Entsorgung radioaktiver Abfälle eine Stellungnahme zum Entsorgungsbericht'88*, "NVwZ" 1989, p. 1116.
11 H.Koch, A.Roβnagel, Neue *Energiepolitik und Ausstieg aus der Kernenergie*, "NVwZ" 2000, p. 8; B.Bonin, *Jak postępować* . . . , p. 690.
12 C.Offermann, *Die Entsorgung* . . . , p. 1116.
13 Bundesminister des Innern, *Antwort* . . . , p. 9.
14 BVerfGE104,238, p. 240.
15 Ibid.
16 C.Offermann, *Die Entsorgung* . . . , p. 1116.
17 Bundesminister des Innern, *Antwort* . . . , p. 10.
18 B.Bonin, *Jak postępować* . . . , s. 688–689.
19 Bundesminister des Innern, *Antwort* . . . , p. 10.
20 B.Bonin, *Jak postępować* . . . , s. 690.
21 Ibid.
22 Ibid.
23 C.Offermann, *Die Entsorgung* . . . , p. 1116.
24 Bundesminister des Innern, *Antwort* . . . , p. 10.
25 Ibid.
26 H.Koch, A.Roβnagel, *Neue Energiepolitik* . . . , p. 8.
27 Translation based on: P.Becker, *Aufstieg und Krise der deutschen Stromkonzerne*, Bochum 2011, p. 353.
28 *Übereinkommen über nukleare Sicherheit. Bericht der Bundesrepublik Deutschland für die Sechste Überprüfungstagung im März/April 2014, Bonn 2013*, p. 192; H.Koch, A.Roβnagel, *Neue Energiepolitik* . . . , p. 8.
29 *Übereinkommen* . . . , p. 179.
30 Ibid.
31 Ibid.
32 Ibid.
33 Ibid.
34 Ibid.
35 O.Däuper, A.Bernstorff, *Gesetz* . . . , p. 24.
36 Publ. BGBl. 2011 I p. 1704.
37 See FCC's judgment of 12 November 2008, ref. 1 BvR 2456/06. www.bundesverfassungsgericht.de/SharedDocs/Entscheidungen/DE/2008/11/rk20081112_1bvr245606.html; also published in: *BVerfG: Standortzwischenlager für Kernbrennstoffe – Grafenrheinfeld*, "NVwZ" 2009, pp. 171–176; further references to individual passages of this judgment will follow the electronic version available on the above-mentioned website of the FCC.
38 See FCC's judgment of 12 November 2008, ref. 1 BvR 2456/06, §1.

39 Twelve interim storage facilities are in operation, but thirteen were planned at the time.
40 Ibid., §12.
41 Ibid.
42 Ibid.
43 Ibid.
44 Ibid., §13.
45 Ibid.
46 Ibid.
47 Ibid.
48 Ibid., §15.
49 Ibid., §19.
50 Ibid., §27.
51 Ibid., §25.
52 Ibid.
53 So FCC in its judgment of 12 November 2008, ref. 1 BvR 2456/06, §25.
54 Ibid., §27.
55 Ibid.
56 Ibid.
57 Ibid., §§28–71.
58 Ibid.
59 Ibid., §30.
60 Ibid., §31.
61 Ibid.
62 Ibid.
63 Emphasis directly after FCC.
64 So FCC in its judgment of 12 November 2008, ref. 1 BvR 2456/06, §31.
65 Ibid., §32.
66 Ibid.
67 Ibid., §58.
68 Ibid.
69 Ibid.
70 Ibid., §59.
71 Ibid.
72 See judgment of the Federal Administrative Court (*Bundesverwaltungsgericht*) of 14 January 1998, ref. BverwG 11 C 11.96, publ. *BVerwG: Aufhebung einer atomrechtlichen Betriebsgenehmigung – Obrigheim*, "NVwZ" 1998, p. 628 et seq.; judgment of the Federal Administrative Court of 19 January 1989, ref. BVerG 7 C 31.87, publ. *BVerwG: Bewaffneter Werkschutz im Kernkraftwerk* "NVwZ" 1989, pp. 864 et seq.
73 So FCC in its judgment of 12 November 2008, ref. 1 BvR 2456/06, §67.
74 Ibid., §67.
75 Ibid.
76 Ibid.
77 Ibid., §68.
78 Ibid.
79 Ibid., §33.
80 Ibid., §35.
81 Ibid.
82 Ibid.

83 Ibid., §62.
84 Ibid.
85 Ibid.
86 Ibid.
87 Ibid.
88 Ibid.
89 Ibid.
90 Opposite view presented i.a. by P.Hocke, A.Brunnengräber, *Multi-Level Governance of Nuclear Waste Disposal* [in:] A.Brunnengräber, M.Di Nucci (eds.), *Conflicts . . .*
91 Ibid., §35.
92 M.Schmidt-Preuβ, *Das neue Atomrecht*, "NVwZ" 1998, pp. 557–558.
93 Ibid., p. 557.
94 Ibid., pp. 557–558.
95 Ibid., p. 558.
96 H.Koch, A.Roβnagel, *Neue Energiepolitik . . .* , p. 9.
97 J.Kuhbier, U.Prall, *Errichtung . . .* , p. 361.
98 Ibid.
99 Ibid.
100 However it was recently merged into the 100% state-owned company: *Bundesgesellschaft für Endlagerung* (BGE).
101 Ibid., p. 358.
102 Ibid.
103 J.Kuhbier, U.Prall, *Errichtung . . .* , p. 358.
104 M.Schmidt-Preuβ, *Das neue Atomrecht . . .* , s. 557.
105 J.Kuhbier, U.Prall, *Errichtung . . .* , pp. 358–359.
106 Ibid., p. 359.
107 Ibid.
108 Ibid.
109 Ibid.
110 Ibid.
111 Ibid.
112 Ibid.
113 Ibid.
114 Ibid.
115 Ibid.
116 M.Schmidt-Preuβ, *Das neue Atomrecht . . .* , p. 558.
117 H.Gaβner, J.Kendzia, *Atomrechtliche Staatshaftung und die Zustimmungsbedürftigkeit der 11. AtG-Novelle,* "ZUR" 2010, vol. 12, p. 458.
118 M.Schmidt-Preuβ, *Das neue Atomrecht . . .* , p. 558.
119 H.Gaβner, J.Kendzia, *Atomrechtliche Staatshaftung . . .* , p. 457.
120 Ibid.
121 Ibid.
122 C.Ziehm, *Sicherstellung der Finanzierungsvorsorge für den Rückbau der Atomkraftwerke und die Entsorgung radioaktiver Abfälle*, "ZUR" 2015, pp. 658–659.
123 G.Volk, *Der Ausstieg aus der Atomkraft und die Rückstellungsproblematik*, "Deutsches Steuerrecht" 2015, pp. 2195–2196.
124 Ibid.
125 Ibid., p. 2196.
126 Ibid.
127 Ibid.

128 Ibid.
129 Ibid.
130 Ibid.
131 Ibid.
132 C.Ziehm, *Sicherstellung* . . . , p. 658.
133 Ibid.
134 Ibid.
135 G.Volk, *Der Ausstieg* . . . , p. 2196.
136 Ibid., pp. 2196–2197.
137 C.Ziehm, *Sicherstellung* . . . , pp. 658–659.
138 Ibid., p. 659.
139 Ibid.
140 H.Schmitz, H.Grefrath, *Die Neujustierung der Vorsorge für die Stilllegung der Kernkraftwerke – Stiftung oder Entsorgungsfonds?* "Neue Verwaltungszeitschrift" 2015, p. 169.
141 G.Volk, *Der Ausstieg* . . . , p. 2195.
142 H.Schmitz, H.Grefrath, *Die Neujustierung* . . . , p. 169.
143 See inter alia C.Ziehm, *Sicherstellung* . . . , p. 659; G.Volk, *Der Ausstieg* . . . , p. 2193 ff.; H.Schmitz, H.Grefrath, *Die Neujustierung* . . . , p. 169 ff.
144 G.Volk, *Der Ausstieg* . . . , p. 2193.
145 C.Ziehm, *Sicherstellung* . . . , p. 663.
146 Ibid.
147 H.Schmitz, H.Grefrath, *Die Neujustierung* . . . , p. 170.
148 See Information available on the RAG-Stiftung website: <www.rag-stiftung.de/ueber-uns/>.
149 See Information available online on the website of Evonik Industries AG, the legal successor of RAG AG: <http://geschichte.evonik.de/sites/geschichte/de/gesellschaften/evonik-industries/Pages/default.aspx>.
150 C.Ziehm, *Sicherstellung* . . . , p. 663.
151 Ibid.
152 Ibid.
153 Ibid.
154 RAG-Stiftung, *Konzernlagebericht der RAG-Stiftung für das Geschäftsjahr 2011*, p. 21. <www.rag-stiftung.de/fileadmin/user_upload/RAG-Stiftung_Konzernabschluss_2011.pdf>.
155 Ibid., p. 12.
156 RAG-Stiftung, *Konzernlagebericht der RAG-Stiftung für das Geschäftsjahr 2016*, p. 33. <www.rag-stiftung.de/fileadmin/user_upload/RAG-Stiftung_Gescha__ttsbericht_2016_FINAL.pdf>.
157 Ibid., p. 21.
158 C.Ziehm, *Sicherstellung*, p. 663.
159 H.Schmitz, H.Grefrath, *Die Neujustierung* . . . , p. 170.
160 C.Ziehm, *Sicherstellung* . . . , p. 663–664.
161 H.Schmitz, H.Grefrath, *Die Neujustierung* . . . , p. 169.
162 As stated in: H.Schmitz, H.Grefrath, *Die Neujustierung* . . . , p. 170.
163 G.Volk, *Der Ausstieg* . . . , p. 2195.
164 H.Schmitz, H.Grefrath, *Die Neujustierung* . . . , p. 170.
165 A different view is expressed by H.Schmitz, H.Grefrath in *Die Neujustierung* . . . , p. 170. They say that the receipts from the power plant will be high enough for the new foundation.
166 C.Ziehm, *Sicherstellung* . . . , p. 664.

167 Ibid.
168 H.Schmitz, H.Grefrath, *Die Neujustierung . . .* , p. 170.
169 Cf. M.Kloepfer, *Verfahrene Atomausstiegsverfahren? – Verfahrensfragen bei der Ausstiegsgesetzgebung im Atomrecht*, "Umwelt und Planungsrecht" 2012, no. 2, p. 41 et seq.
170 See M.Kloepfer, D.Bruch, *Die Laufzeitverlängerung im Atomrecht zwischen Gesetz und Vertrag*, "Juristen Zeitung" 2011, p. 377–387.
171 F.Schorkopf, *Die „vereinbarte" Novellierung des Atomgesetzes*, "Neue Verwaltungszeitschrift" 2000, p. 1112 [as cited in:] H.Schmitz, H.Grefrath, *Die Neujustierung . . .* , p. 170.
172 H.Schmitz, H.Grefrath, *Die Neujustierung . . .* , p. 170.
173 G.Volk, *Der Ausstieg . . .* , p. 2195.
174 C.Ziehm, *Sicherstellung . . .* , p. 658.
175 Ibid.
176 C.Ziehm, *Sicherstellung . . .* , p. 658.
177 Ibid., p. 664.
178 H.Schmitz, H.Grefrath, *Die Neujustierung . . .* , p. 170.
179 Ibid.
180 Ibid., p. 174.
181 G.Volk, *Der Ausstieg . . .* , p. 2195.
182 H.Schmitz, H.Grefrath, *Die Neujustierung . . .* , p. 174.
183 Ibid.
184 Ibid.
185 Ibid., p. 175.
186 Ibid.
187 Ibid.
188 Ibid.
189 Ibid.
190 Ibid.
191 Ibid.
192 Ibid.
193 Ibid.
194 Ibid., p. 171.
195 Ibid., pp. 172–173.
196 Ibid., p. 173.
197 Ibid.
198 Draft dated 9 November 2015, publ. Deutscher Bundestag 18. Wahlperiode Drucksache 18/6615, hereafter *Rückbau- und EntsorgungskostennachhaftungsG*. <http://dip21.bundestag.de/dip21/btd/18/066/1806615.pdf>.
199 See the Justification to the Act Rückbau- und Entsorgungskostennachhaftungs G, p. 1.
200 Ibid.
201 Ibid., p. 7.
202 Ibid., p. 1.
203 Ibid., p. 10.
204 Ibid., p. 11.
205 As stated in Justification to the Act Rückbau- und Entsorgungskostennachhaftungs G, p. 7.
206 Ibid.
207 Ibid.

208 Published in: BGBl. I No. 5, p. 114.

209 This analysis can also include commercial reactors that are no longer in use and are in the process of being decommissioned, as well as those that have already been decommissioned because they have high-level radioactive waste left behind. The scope of the bill will therefore include these entities as well.

210 See i.a. M.Calleja, S.Borg, *Piercing the corporate veil: Greening companies' governance and shareholder activism*, "IUCNAEL E-Journal" 2017, vol. 7, p. 36–56.

211 See *Übereinkommen über nukleare Sicherheit. Bericht der Bundesrepublik Deutschland für die Fünfte Überprüfungstagung im April 2011*, Bonn 2010, p. 204; as of 4 August 2010.

212 Ibid., p. 205; as of 4 August 2010.

213 Ibid., pp. 206–208; as of 4 August 2010.

References

Alley W., Alley R., *Too hot to touch. The problem of high-level nuclear waste*, Cambridge 2012.

Becker P., *Aufstieg und Krise der deutschen Stromkonzerne*, Bochum 2011.

BMU, *Übereinkommen über nukleare Sicherheit. Bericht der Bundesrepublik Deutschland für die Fünfte Überprüfungstagung im April 2011*, Bonn 2010.

Bonin B., *Jak postępować z odpadami jądrowymi?* [in:] K.Jeleń, Z.Rau (eds.), *Energetyka jądrowa w Polsce*, Warsaw 2012.

Brunnengräber A., *The "wicked problem" of long term radioactive waste governance* [in:] A.Brunnengräber, M.Di Nucci (eds.), *Conflicts, participation and acceptability in nuclear waste governance*, Wiesbaden 2019.

Bundesminister des Innern, *Antwort der Bundesregierung auf die Große Anfrage der Abgeordneten Dr. Laufs, Dr. Dregger, Spranger, Dr. Riesenhuber, Dr. Miltner, Lenzer, Broll, Fellner, Dr. von Geldern, Gerlach, Dr. Waffenschmidt, Dr. Bugl, Gerstein, Frau Hürland, Kolb, Dr. George, Dr. Jobst, Dr. Köhler (Wolfsburg), Dr. Kunz (Weiden), Magin, Pfeffermann, Prangenberg, Schwarz, Dr. Stavenhagen und der Fraktion der CDU/CSU – Drucksache 9/858 – Verantwortung des Bundes für Sicherstellung und Endlagerung radioaktiver Abfälle in der Bundesrepublik Deutschland* of 22 December 1981, „Deutscher Bundestag Drucksache 9/1231", pp. 1–14.

BVerfG: Standortzwischenlager für Kernbrennstoffe – Grafenrheinfeld, "NVwZ" 2009, pp. 171–176.

BVerwG: Aufhebung einer atomrechtlichen Betriebsgenehmigung – Obrigheim, „NVwZ" 1998, pp. 623–628.

BVerwG: Bewaffneter Werkschutz im Kernkraftwerk "NVwZ" 1989, pp. 864 et seq.

Calleja M., Borg S., *Piercing the corporate veil: Greening Companies' Governance and Shareholder Activism*, "IUCNAEL E-Journal" 2017, vol. 7, pp. 36–56. www.iucnael.org/en/documents/1296-piercing-the-corporate-veil.

Däuper O., Bernstorff A., *Gesetz zur Suche und Auswahl eines Standortes für die Endlagerung radioaktiver Abfälle – zugleich ein Vorschlag für die Agenda der „Kommission Lagerung hoch radioaktiver Abfallstoffe"*, „ZUR" 2014, pp. 24–32.

Drögemüller C., *Schlüsselakteure der Endlager-Governance. Entsorgungsoptionen und – strategien radioaktiver Abfälle aus Sicht regionaler Akteure*, Wiesbaden 2018.

Erichsen H., Martens W. (eds.), *Allgemeines Verwaltungsrecht*, Berlin 1995.

Faber H., *Verwaltungsrecht*, Tübingen 1989.

Gaβner H., Kendzia J., *Atomrechtliche Staatshaftung und die Zustimmungsbedürftigkeit der 11. AtG-Novelle*, "ZUR" 2010, vol. 12, pp. 456–460.

Haedrich H., *Zur Zulässigkeit der Wiederaufarbeitung abgebrannter Brennelemente aus deutschen Kernkraftwerken in anderen EG-Mitgliedstaaten* "NVwZ" 1993, pp. 1036–1044.

Hocke P., Brunnengräber A., *Multi-level governance of nuclear waste disposal* [in:] A.Brunnengräber, M.Di Nucci (eds.), *Conflicts, participation and acceptability in nuclear waste governance*, Wiesbaden 2019.

Kloepfer M., *Verfahrene Atomausstiegsverfahren? – Verfahrensfragen bei der Ausstiegsgesetzgebung im Atomrecht*, „Umwelt und Planungsrecht" 2012, No. 2, p. 41 et seq.

Kloepfer M., Bruch D., *Die Laufzeitverlängerung im Atomrecht zwischen Gesetz und Vertrag*, „Juristen Zeitung" 2011, pp. 377–387.

Koch H., Roβnagel A., *Neue Energiepolitik und Ausstieg aus der Kernenergie*, "NVwZ" 2000, p. 1 et seq.

Kuhbier J., Prall U., *Errichtung und Betrieb von Endlagern für radioaktive Abfälle durch Beliehene?*, „ZUR" 2009, vol. 7–8, pp. 358–364.

Kunig P. (ed.), *Grundgesetz-Kommentar. Band 2*, München 1995.

Maurer H., *Allgemeines Verwaltungsrecht*, München 2011.

Offermann C., *Die Entsorgung radioaktiver Abfälle eine Stellungnahme zum Entsorgungsbericht'88*, "NVwZ" 1989, pp. 1112–1120.

Olliges J., *A "deliberative turn" in German nuclear waste governance?* [in:] A.Brunnengräber, M.Di Nucci (eds.), *Conflicts, participation and acceptability in nuclear waste governance*, Wiesbaden 2019.

Palandt O. (ed.), *Bürgerliches Gesetzbuch*, München 2011.

RAG-Stiftung, *Konzernlagebericht der RAG-Stiftung für das Geschäftsjahr 2011*, RAG-Stiftung 2012. www.rag-stiftung.de/fileadmin/user_upload/RAG-Stiftung_Konzernabschluss_2011.pdf

RAG-Stiftung, *Konzernlagebericht der RAG-Stiftung für das Geschäftsjahr 2016*, RAG-Stiftung 2017. www.rag-stiftung.de/fileadmin/user_upload/RAG-Stiftung_Gescha__ftsbericht_2016_FINAL.pdf

Ramana M., *Why technical solutions are insufficient. The abiding conundrum of nuclear waste* [in:] A.Brunnengräber, M.Di Nucci (eds.), *Conflicts, participation and acceptability in nuclear waste governance*, Wiesbaden 2019.

Schmidt-Preuβ M., *Das neue Atomrecht*, „NVwZ" 1998, pp. 553–562.

Schmitz H., Grefrath H., *Die Neujustierung der Vorsorge für die Stilllegung der Kernkraftwerke – Stiftung oder Entsorgungsfonds?* „Neue Verwaltungszeitschrift" 2015, pp. 169–176.

Schorkopf F., *Die „vereinbarte" Novellierung des Atomgesetzes*, „NVwZ" 2000, p. 1111 et seq.

Staudinger J., *Kommentar zum Bürgerlichen Gesetzbuch mit Einführungsgeetz und Nebengesetzen. Buch 2. Recht der Schuldverhältnisse §§ 839, 839a (Unerlaubte Handlungen 4 – Amtshaftungsrecht)*, Berlin 2007.

Übereinkommen über nukleare Sicherheit. Bericht der Bundesrepublik Deutschland für die Fünfte Überprüfungstagung im April 2011, Bonn 2010.

Übereinkommen über nukleare Sicherheit. Bericht der Bundesrepublik Deutschland für die Sechste Überprüfungstagung im März/April 2014, Bonn 2013.Ulmer P. (ed.), *Münchener Kommentar zum Bürgerlichen Gesetzbuch. Band 5. Schuldrecht. Besonderer Teil III*, München 1997.

Vogt M., *Zur ethischen Bewertung der Atomenergie nach Tschernobyl und Fukushima* [in:] J.Ostheimer, M.Vogt (eds.), *Die Moral der Energiewende. Risikowhrnehmung im Wandel m Beispiel der Atomenergie*, Stuttgart 2014.

Volk G., *Der Ausstieg aus der Atomkraft und die Rückstellungsproblematik*, „Deutsches Steurrecht" 2015, p. 2193 et seq.

Wollenteit U., *Gorleben und kein Ende*, "ZUR" 2014, pp. 323–329.

Ziehm C., *Sicherstellung der Finanzierungsvorsorge für den Rückbau der Atomkraftwerke und die Entsorgung radioaktiver Abfälle*, „ZUR" 2015, pp. 658–664.

3 Selection of a proper site for final disposal of radioactive waste

A kind of culmination of the German state's efforts to manage and neutralise radioactive waste is how it deals with the problem of radioactive waste disposal. This public task, which remains unresolved to this day, has been incumbent upon the Federation ever since the German state decided to begin the peaceful use of nuclear energy, accompanied by corresponding amendments to the Basic Law in 1959 and the concurrent enactment of Atomic Law.

An indication of how far the issue is from being resolved is that the efforts to establish a procedure to select a location for a radioactive waste final disposal facility and its appropriate technology are currently underway. This work is not very advanced, which shows the complexity of the matter at hand. In turn, such painstaking elaboration on how to reach a decision in this area demonstrates how controversial the issue is from a societal perspective.

On 23 July 2013, a federal law was enacted on searching for and selecting the location of a radioactive waste disposal facility (commonly known as: *Standortauswahlgesetz*). The law was subject to a major overhaul in 2017 – a new statute was adopted[1] under the same title. It is worth examining both statutes in terms of the institutional solutions they provide and the principles of substantive constitutional law cited in their justification. It can be hypothesised that the 2013 and 2017 *Standortauswahlgesetz* reflect the essence of the achievements of the German democratic constitutional system – as they provide the institutional framework for a long-standing social discussion. The 2013-*Standortauswahlgesetz* was originally scheduled to take 18 years to implement, with the main goal of definitively solving the nuclear waste management problem for at least a million years. Although an overall assessment of the effectiveness of 2013 and 2017 *Standortauswahlgesetz* will only be possible after the 18 years in question have elapsed, it will already be possible to make a preliminary assessment of its usefulness in practice today on the basis of initial experience with its introduction.

DOI: 10.4324/9781003198086-4

1. Initial selection of Gorleben as a site for the radioactive waste disposal facility

According to §9a(3) sentence 1 of Atomic Law, the Federation is required to establish and then operate a radioactive waste final disposal facility. This obligation was imposed on the Federation in 1976 with the so-called 4th Amendment to Atomic Law.[2] Already on the 22 February 1977 the disused Gorleben salt mine in Lower Saxony was named as a possible site.[3] The Federation had been working in Gorleben since 1979 to adapt it to this task.[4] However, the choice of Gorleben as the location for the radioactive waste disposal facility was made in a manner unknown to the general public.[5] Precise selection criteria have never been published.[6] The basis for that technical process carried out at the time was the Mining Law, which did not provide for any form of public participation.[7]

Rather, an analysis of selected Federal government documents confirms this is what the Federal Government was doing in this matter.[8] Geological investigations (primarily drillings in target deposits) of other alternative locations for a radioactive waste disposal facility have not been conducted.[9] Rock formations other than salt[10] deposits have not been studied because of their suitability for use as a final disposal facility.[11] Not surprisingly, the subject of criticism in both the literature and public debate has been the presentation of the Gorleben location as the only possible one. The official government position on the suitability of Gorleben as a disposal site was maintained by federal authorities until 1998.[12] However, more recent sources reconstructing the decision made at the time to choose Gorleben indicate that several other locations were also considered.[13] There has even been preliminary research work as to their suitability.[14] In contrast, the factor that may have determined the choice of Gorleben was political,[15] or even economic.[16] Gorleben was located right on the border with the German Democratic Republic, which had begun construction of its own radioactive waste disposal facility a dozen years earlier, also in the border area.[17] Although the thesis that the choice of Gorleben location was determined by political and economic considerations[18] could shed more light on the reasons why the choice of Gorleben location went the way it did, it is disputed because it cannot be unequivocally confirmed.[19] Another political factor should be also pointed out, consisting of local politicians blocking the originally chosen sites (even before Gorleben).[20]

It is worthwhile to describe the atmosphere of the discussion that took place at that time. Gorleben had become the most iconic symbol for opponents of nuclear power.[21] They went quite far in their argument against the Gorleben site, pointing out that reports of alleged progress on the disposal facility were only to serve as an alibi for the nuclear industry. Allegedly, the idea was to extend the life of nuclear reactors as much as possible, but not to solve the issue of management and neutralisation of the nuclear waste generated.[22] On the other hand, the mass protests around Gorleben were also intended to block further development of nuclear power in Germany by making it impossible to resolve the issue of radioactive waste.[23]

One element of the political compromise resulting from *Atomausstieg I* was the agreement that work to prepare the Gorleben site would cease and the search for another location for the central radioactive waste disposal facility would begin.[24] Accordingly the provisions of Part IV, Section 4 of the contract of 14 June 2000 between the Federal Government and the energy companies provided for the interruption of research work at the Gorleben site for a minimum of three years and a maximum of ten years "until doubts about the concept of the planned radioactive waste disposal facility and safety are clarified".[25] At the same time, an important part of the 2000 agreement was the "Federation Statement on Exploration of the Gorleben Rock Salt Deposit".[26] In the Statement, the Federal Government indicated that numerous doubts had arisen as to whether the rock salt deposits at the Gorleben site could be used according to the accepted technique, and the period of suspension of work at the Gorleben site was intended to clarify these doubts. At the same time, the Federal Government has made it clear that it was not abandoning the Gorleben site. These declarations amounted to a de facto moratorium on further work to adapt Gorleben into a radioactive waste disposal facility for the whole of Germany. The moratorium was implemented immediately.[27]

At the same time, the matter in question was the subject of a ruling by the Federal Constitutional Court. The moratorium was challenged in court by the Land of Bavaria.[28] It should be noted that Bavaria had a keen interest in the subject matter, as it is home to several nuclear reactors (including radioactive waste left over from years of operation) and is also the seat of the local government company Stadtwerke München, a shareholder in one of the largest nuclear reactors in Germany. The motion to the FCC by Bavaria initiated proceedings in the form of a competence dispute between the Federation and the Länder.[29] The dispute concerned whether the constitutional principle of good cooperation within the federal state *(Grundsatz des bundesfreundlichen Verhaltens*) should imply a prohibition on the Federation not to proceed with the adaptation of Gorleben to become a site for radioactive waste disposal facility and not to interrupt the implementation of the so-called "integrated concept for the disposal of radioactive waste" without the participation of the Länder[30] (decision by representatives of the Federal Government and the Länder on 28 September 1979),[31] i.e. plans to establish a radioactive waste disposal facility at Gorleben, as well as the world's largest reprocessing facility for spent nuclear fuel.[32] The Land of

Bavaria attempted to show that §9a(3) sentence 1 of Atomic Law is to be derived from the Federation's obligation to permanently conduct efficient work on the final disposal facility.[33] The special relationship of the Federation with the Länder in the area of radioactive waste is to result from the division of administration between the Federation and the Länder. The Federation has responsibilities for the final disposal facility, while the Länder have responsibilities for the interim storage of radioactive waste, an obligation mandated by the Federation.[34] From this combination of administrative tasks, it follows that the Federation and the Länder have a strong, multi-level interconnection.[35] Meanwhile, the federal moratorium decision taken is an example of shifting the burden of responsibility for radioactive waste management to the Länder. The Federation is thus shifting responsibility in this regard away from itself for a long time. The appellant pointed out that the Federation's policy on radioactive waste to date has been in concert with the Länder.[36] The principle of good federal-state cooperation, according to the Appellant, even implies its compulsion. Therefore, the unilateral abandonment by the Federation of the hitherto implemented integrated concept of management and disposal of radioactive waste is to constitute a violation of the principle of good cooperation within the federal state.[37]

In connection with the competence dispute, the Federal Government stated that the decision of 28 September 1979, was merely a political confirmation of the Federal Government's conception of the disposal of radioactive waste at the time.[38] Since then, significant changes have taken place: the projects to build fast breeder reactors and systems to reprocess nuclear fuel at Wackersdorf have been abandoned. In addition, the reprocessing of spent fuel was equated by statute with direct disposal.[39] The Federal Government stated that the moratorium is justified, but that Bavaria, as a Land, has no authority to question its effects. According to the position of the Federal Government, interim storage is the responsibility of the nuclear reactor operators, while the Länder are only required to conduct construction licensing proceedings, as well as exercise day-to-day supervision of the reactors.[40] Only that the obligations incumbent upon the Länder are derived from mandated tasks under Atomic Law, and their costs are borne by the Federation in accordance with the provision of Article 104a(2) of *Grundgesetz*.[41]

The FCC ruled that Bavaria, as a Land, is not entitled to the legitimate demand under the Basic Law that the Federation continuously carry out efficient work on the radioactive waste disposal facility.[42] The Court found that there was no right for the appellant to request to participate in making changes to the concept of radioactive waste management and disposal.[43] No new constitutionally established legal position vis-à-vis the Federation arises for the appellant from the combined (and interrelated) performance of administrative tasks by both the Federation and the Länder.[44] Ultimately, in the Court's view, the Federation, which at that time had competing legislative competence to make changes to the concept of disposal of radioactive waste, did not violate the principle of the division of powers between the Federation and the Länder or the principle of good cooperation within the federal state.[45] The qualified decision of 28 September 1979, in the Court's view, had only political significance, i.e[46] it had no legal force. The FCC pointed out that this decision was merely a subsequent confirmation of a particular concept for the disposal of radioactive waste, which was then already entrenched in the law.[47] The Court stated about taking the appropriate decision at that time as a result of political opportunism.[48]

2. Selecting a new location for a radioactive waste disposal facility

During the period of the moratorium referred to in the passage quoted above, legislative work was underway to put in place an appropriate legislative framework. In June 2005, the first draft of a bill to establish the location of a radioactive waste disposal facility was prepared.[49] At the same time, the Bundestag elections of 18 September 2005 brought this law[50] to an end (due to the principle of the discontinuation of parliamentary work). Subsequently, due to the so-called *Laufzeitverlängerung*, the moratorium was lifted and work resumed on the Gorleben site.[51] The Fukushima disaster, which resulted in the so-called *Atomausstieg II*, opened a "window of opportunity"[52] that enabled restarting the whole process.[53] This resulted in a cross-party resolution to work out in a joint committee of the Federation and the Länder a procedure for selecting a site other than Gorleben for a final disposal facility.[54] It was the result of this work that on 23 July 2013 a federal law (*Standortauswahlgesetz*) was passed on how to search for and select a site for a radioactive waste disposal facility.[55] The 2013-*Standortauswahlgesetz* did not provide a ready-made solution but established a procedure to develop those solutions. It would follow that this resolution should be read as an attempt to fill the existing legitimacy deficit of the radioactive waste disposal site selection proceedings.[56]

The explanatory memorandum for this law cites the compromise reached in connection with *Atomausstieg II*. At the same time, the Act itself is, in a way, an attempt to extend that compromise[57] by implementing to high-level radioactive waste management the findings on which that compromise was built. This approach (most probably) is based on lessons learnt that managing radioactive waste is not just a technical, but also a social challenge.[58] In fact, according to the Act's proponents, the process of finding a location for a disposal facility for medium- and high-level radioactive waste is supposed to be an opportunity to develop a national compromise.[59] The explanatory memorandum to the Act says that such a compromise must be worked out along three dimensions. First, between the Federation and the Länder. Second, between the state and society. Third, a compromise is also to be reached among citizens.[60]

Firstly, one ought to consider what would result from a compromise between the Federation and the Länder. Following the reform of the Basic Law *(Föderalismusreform)*, since 2006 the Federation has had exclusive legislative competence in the field of nuclear energy, including with regard to the location of a final disposal facility for radioactive waste. However, a disposal facility for radioactive (high-level) waste will be built on the territory of a specific Land. Undoubtedly, having a final disposal facility for radioactive waste from the entire Federal Republic of Germany (not only new waste, but also waste generated over nearly 70 years of nuclear power) in one's area can detract from a Land's attractiveness to others.[61] Other Lands will thus be in an advantageous position, as they will not have such a disposal facility on their territory and will not be exposed to appropriate risks.[62]

The second dimension of compromise referred to in *Standortauswahlgesetz* is the development of an agreement between the state and society. The radioactive waste disposal facility in Gorleben was abandoned against a backdrop of conflict between the state and the public. It would be an overgeneralisation to say that the issue of radioactive waste conflated the entire society with the state, but there was certainly a kind of polarisation of society around the Gorleben issue. In fact, a large part of it opposed the Gorleben site, and the intensity of the protests was said to resemble a civil war.[63] The Green Party (Grünen/Bündnis'90), today the second political force in Germany, was founded on the basis of protests against nuclear energy, which focused on the issue of radioactive waste.

Standortauswahlgesetz was intended to be an attempt to forge a compromise among citizens themselves due to the polarisation of society regarding nuclear power. This attempt has already been assessed as "the most extensive and long-lasting participatory experiment in German history".[64] Since an initial compromise on nuclear waste disposal has been reached on the political level, this may be the right time to reduce the polarisation of society and resolve the accumulated social conflicts. This coincides with the "Integrationsprinzip" stressed in the case law of the FCC.[65]

3. Lawmakers' decision to expand list of potential sites to include Gorleben

Working out a compromise between the state and society, however, can be disrupted. Paradoxically, *Standortauswahlgesetz* did not rule out Gorleben as a possible location for high-level radioactive waste final disposal facility from across the Federation[66] – allegedly as a compromise between the Federal Government and Länder.[67] Moreover, §21 of *Standortauswahlgesetz* requires that this location be taken into account from the outset. It is made clear in the rationale that this is not to be a reference location, however.[68] This is to be determined only if it is unequivocally ruled out at some stage in the selection of a site for the final disposal facility. This approach to Gorleben (with all the experience associated with that location) is considered in the literature to be a huge mistake of the lawmaker.[69] It should be noted that the point of the proceedings on the selection of the site for high-level radioactive waste final disposal facility has so far been precisely to consider locations other than Gorleben.[70] However, the consideration of the Gorleben location is supposed to be due to the so-called "white map" ("blank map" or "blank slate") approach[71] and the circumstance that it is scientifically impossible to rule out a predetermined location.[72]

Nevertheless, the consideration of Gorleben location does not necessarily invalidate all efforts to forge a compromise between state and society. After all, it cannot be ruled out that the Gorleben location will not turn out to be the best possible one after all. The public debate in Germany about radioactive waste and its disposal at Gorleben has been going on for decades. Gorleben was negatively exposed enough at the time, so it is unlikely that this location is chosen. This is a paradox, because a law was prepared with a separate mode to just move away from the Gorleben site and find another location. It may also be that even if the Gorleben site ultimately proved to be the best, it will not be chosen because it was not for the statutory effort that the site was ultimately chosen again. It is unlikely that even such a transparent process as the *Standortauswahlgesetz* would have succeeded in overcoming the public resistance to the Gorleben site, even if it had turned out to be the best location. What is needed is the need for society to overcome past conflicts.[73] Experience during the period of the HLRWD-Commission's work also indicates that the statutory obligation to take the Gorleben location into account had a significant negative impact on the HLRWD-Commission's work.[74] Any criteria developed for the new location resulted in a reference to Gorleben. This, of course, disturbed the neutrality of establishing criteria for selecting the location and technology of a radioactive waste disposal facility.[75] Hence, there were demands to exclude the Gorleben location from further work carried out on the basis of 2013-*Standortauswahlgesetz*.[76]

The 2013-*Standortauswahlgesetz's* retention of the Gorleben site as one of the potential locations for a radioactive waste disposal facility may be due to financial issues. Until now, energy companies that have generated radioactive waste have paid fees to cover the cost of a radioactive waste disposal facility *(Endlagervorausleistung)*.[77] By the year 2000, nearly four billion Deutschmarks had already been collected from energy companies for the realisation of a disposal site at the Gorleben (high-level radioactive waste) and Konrad (low-level radioactive waste) locations.[78] This was based on §21b(4) of Atomic Law.[79] This regulation implies that the companies are not entitled to a refund of fees paid if, for substantive reasons, the plans for a particular disposal site are not implemented.[80] This issue is also referred to in Part 4, Section 7 of the contract of 14 June 2000 between the Federal Government and the energy companies within the framework of *Atomausstieg I*,[81] which related to the costs already incurred for the Gorleben site and the Konrad shaft. According to the agreement, the costs to date were considered to "represent necessary expenditures".[82] At the same time, the energy companies have undertaken not to claim reimbursement for the costs incurred for the Gorleben site as a disposal facility for high-level radioactive waste and for their share of the costs incurred for the Konrad shaft as a disposal for low- and intermediate-level radioactive waste.[83] The waiver to seek any costs from the Federation was based on the Federation's promise to secure the Gorleben location during the moratorium period.[84]

Meanwhile, the essence of *Standortauswahlgesetz* is to start anew with the selection of a location for a high-level radioactive waste disposal facility.[85] The temporary moratorium from *Atomausstieg I* changes to an indefinite moratorium, although since the Gorleben location has not been ruled out (on the contrary), this moratorium can be lifted. *Standortauswahlgesetz's* discontinuation of existing measures also means that money already spent for this purpose is partially wasted. Moreover, *Standortauswahlgesetz*, in defining the level of outlays that the national economy will have to bear in connection with the implementation of this law, indicates that entities obliged to transfer radioactive waste will refinance the administration costs incurred by the Federation in connection with the implementation of this law.[86] These have been estimated at just over two billion euros.[87] Moreover, according to the explanatory memorandum of *Standortauswahlgesetz*, the risk that the Federation will not create and operate a given final disposal facility is supposed to be one of the responsibilities of the entities that generated the radioactive waste.[88] It follows, then, that the risk of the Federation's failure is borne by these entities.

However, it is not clear from the statements of legal scholars whether energy companies would have a claim for reimbursement[89] of the expenses incurred in connection with the *Endlagervorausleistung* if a project was abandoned for purely political reasons. This is why it is conceivable that the rejection of the Gorleben location at *Standortauswahlgesetz* stage could be seen as a purely political act. Then the funds collected as fees from the energy companies would have to be repaid. This is an amount that, if returned and increased by accrued interest due to the loss of value of the money over time, would be substantial. But the legislature's underlying motive appears to be a desire to avoid spending money from the federal government, i.e. taxpayer money, to dispose radioactive waste. This would be contrary to the implementation of "the polluter pays" principle. Politically, the solution would not be defensible in public debate. However, as long as the location of Gorleben is considered equal to other locations during the selection of a disposal facility in connection with *Standortauswahlgesetz*, the risk of no claims for reimbursement of the fees paid will be eliminated.

Most recently BMU announced its decision on closure of the existing nuclear installations in Gorleben as well as withdrawal from any further works on this particular site.[90] Only the incoming years will show whether this decision will stand, but in case it will, this can become a breakthrough for the whole site selection process.

4. Fulfilment by public authorities of their constitutional duties as a justification to adopt the Repository Site Selection Act (*Standortauswahlgesetz*)

The drafters attempted in connection with 2013-*Standortauswahlgesetz* to reconstruct the state's constitutional obligations with respect to the disposal of radioactive waste. According to the Explanatory Memorandum to the Act, the constitutional justification for 2013-*Standortauswahlgesetz* is the obligation of the Federation and the Länder to provide lasting protection for people and the environment from all risks associated with radioactive waste.[91] The project proponents indicated that the solution developed is to apply to future generations as well, as these risks have a very long time horizon.[92] There is also an appeal to the implications of the principle of continuity of state authority. Since the decay period of uranium and plutonium is so long that it exceeds tens of generations, only a state authority can manage radioactive waste, precisely because of the principle of continuity of such authority, among other reasons. In particular, this applies to the duty to protect the health and life of citizens, as well as to care for the environment. In this case, it would mean protecting citizens from the risks of hazards associated with radioactive waste. Such an obligation shall continue to be incumbent upon the Federation and the Länder.

The concept of the law was based on three pillars:[93] 1) priority of safety over any other considerations in doing so, the proceeding conducted is to be based on the findings of science; 2) transparency and fairness of the proceeding in which the location of the final disposal facility will be selected; 3) implementation of "the polluter pays" principle. Each of these pillars simultaneously represents the implementation of particular constitutional provisions.

The priority of safety over all other circumstances means that of the possible solutions, based on the latest findings of science, the only solution to be chosen is the one that will provide the highest level of safety. For example, if one takes into account the fact that radioactive waste involves the risk that geological movements cannot be predicted with certainty, and thus there is the possibility of radioactive waste escaping, for example into drinking water reservoirs, then each choice of the safest solution will realise the constitutional principle of protecting the health and lives of citizens, and will also realise the principle of protecting the environment.

The explanatory memorandum to the bill refers to international regulations in three areas. First, it cites the International Atomic Energy Organization's document of May 2006, *Safety Requirement: Geological Disposal of Radioactive Waste (WS-R-4 2006)* as an international standard for the safe disposal of radioactive waste.[94] This document has been cited as establishing an "indicative framework" and a "minimum standard for Germany".[95] This shows the ambition of the project proponents to create their own highest possible standard. The findings of the International Atomic Energy Organization are therefore rather intended as a guideline in developing proprietary national standards. The explanatory memorandum also points out that the procedure for designating the location of a disposal facility must also meet the standards of the Convention on Nuclear Safety, done at Vienna on 20 September 1994.[96] Germany entered into this international agreement on 13 October 1998.

Finally, the explanatory memorandum to the Act cites the cases of numerous countries as an example of a conducted procedure for selecting the site of final disposal facility for highly radioactive waste.[97] At the same time, proceedings in other countries were to be similarly based on the pillars of adherence to science-based safety standards and meaningful public involvement in the site selection process.[98] Referring to the achievements of other countries, however, can be misleading. This generally applies to countries with much less radioactive waste, such as Finland and Sweden. In addition, these Scandinavian countries are characterised by incomparably lower population density than Germany. In the case of densely populated countries, this means that in the event of a nuclear system accident and the release of nuclear energy or radioactive sources, this limited availability of territory will be further reduced. This will follow the exclusion of the areas concerned as contaminated and the resettlement of the population from the inhabited areas affected by the contamination. Population density also has to do with the impact on the population in the event of any accident. The impact would be incomparably greater in Germany than in Sweden or Finland. And above all, only the German public is so strongly engaged in the public debate related to nuclear power issues. Especially since, from the beginning, the weight of the discussion in Germany also concerned the management and disposal of radioactive waste.

According to §1 of the 2013 and 2017 *Standortauswahlgesetz*, the Act is intended to make possible a procedure that, based on findings of science, is transparent and makes it possible to solve the problem of managing radioactive waste generated in Germany. The procedure under *Standortauswahlgesetz* is to result in indicating the location of the disposal system within the meaning of §9a(3), sentence 1, of Atomic Law.

It is worth noting some of the goals to be achieved in doing so. First of all, the explanatory memorandum to the Act indicates that the process carried out is to be open to different solutions.[99] This is in contrast to the previously pushed concept of locating a disposal facility in Gorleben.[100] At the same time, the explanatory memorandum to the Act stipulates that there are no alternative solutions[101] for the management and disposal of high-level radioactive waste to the selection of the location of the final disposal facility provided for in *Standortauswahlgesetz* and its subsequent construction. This clearly confirms the abandonment of reprocessing of spent fuel.

Another goal of *Standortauswahlgesetz* set forth in §1 is that the selected site will provide safety for at least one million years. The period so designated is absurd in the arbitrariness of selecting one million years as the assumed time of protection. The figure of one million years can be contrasted, first, with the half-life of the elements that predominate in radioactive waste, namely uranium-235 (nearly 700 million years) and plutonium (about 87 years). Second, one million years can be contrasted with the period of modern civilisation (just over two thousand years) or with the period of the Industrial Revolution (about two hundred years). If we juxtapose this with the period of peaceful use of nuclear energy, and if we take 1956 as its beginning due to the commissioning of the first industrial nuclear power plant, which was connected to the public electricity grid at Calder Hall in the UK,[102] it is just over 60 years. Based on only a few decades of experience with the commercial use of nuclear energy worldwide, *Standortauswahlgesetz* contains legal requirements for a level of protection for one million years. Within two to three generations such a waste was generated that will burden ca. 40,000 future generations.[103] This does not mean that such an assumption is incorrect, but the criterion of one million years seems arbitrary. A different perspective on this aspect of *Standortauswahlgesetz* may come from the fact that the drafters intended the one million years to be a measure of ambition of the level of security expected. If such reasons were behind this decision of the legislature, it does not seem appropriate. Today, a given technology may or may not meet a certain level of security according to the best current standard. From the perspective of continued scientific development over the next million years, a given technology may be evaluated quite differently at a later stage of its use. For example, the radiation dose limits will be changed, so some technology today may no longer meet them. Another problem here is that there is an obligation to use contemporary technology that is expected to have a specific effect that is not known to be possible at all. This is because it is inherently impossible to verify radioactive waste disposal technology. This is because only the targeted – and therefore experimental – application will yield the first practical experience.

However, progress is evident at least in the approach to the disposal issue. As recently as 1983, the standard for radioactive waste disposal facilities required that a facility be able to safely store waste for 10,000 years.[104] It is pointed out that such a standard in 1983 was by no means based on real requirements, but on the limited cognitive possibilities at that time compared to the state of the art.[105] It is difficult to consider that a hundredfold increase in cognitive capacity (in the jump from 10,000 to one million years of the required minimum level of protection) has occurred in nearly 40 years. Therefore, it is all the more indicative of how detached from reality the required safety limit of one million years is.

Another possible approach would be to require that once the best technology available today is implemented, it must be continuously adapted to new technical possibilities during its lifetime. For example, such a construction was introduced by Directive 2010/75/EU of the European Parliament and of the Council of 24 November 2010 on industrial emissions (integrated pollution prevention and control).[106] This legal formula, however, is based on the assumption of continuous technological progress in a given area and the administrative forcing of continuous adaptation to this progress by the entities that own the system data covered by this regulation. However, it is hard not to be sceptical about this approach, since for several decades of commercial use of nuclear technology, the only way to neutralise radioactive waste is still to physically separate it from the environment in which humans live, and from the biosphere. In the end there is no absolutely safe disposal technology.[107] In addition, the choice of a legal formula with an obligation to continually adapt to current technology would require selecting a technology that is reversible (allowing radioactive waste to be brought back to the surface). Since there would be an obligation to adapt to new technologies, there would have to be continuous access to this waste (to be able to change the technology used). Meanwhile, some of the techniques used in underground radioactive waste final disposal are based precisely on the lack of retrievability (e.g. due to the expectation that containers of heat-emitting radioactive waste will solidify with the surrounding rock salt).[108]

In addition, *Standortauswahlgesetz* explicitly excludes the possibility of taking radioactive waste outside of Germany for disposal (§1). The explanatory memorandum indicates that the disposal of radioactive waste generated in Germany should be dealt with in the country it was generated, for reasons of national responsibility.[109] This means ruling out any export of radioactive waste. It also shows the implementation in practice of the "polluter pays" constitutional principle. After all, there is no way to escape responsibility for the waste generated by shipping it to a country where the external costs of a disposal facility for that waste would not be considered at all. The provision to leave radioactive waste in Germany means complete transparency about what happens to this waste and the possibility of public control over it, as well as verification of the actual costs incurred and monitoring of its environmental impact. Germany, a member of the G7 and therefore one of the most industrialised countries in the world, has deliberately refused to sell nuclear waste to any developing country, for example.

Furthermore, the aim of *Standortauswahlgesetz* according to §1 is to bring about the selection of the disposal site by 2031. This deadline is due to the expiration in 2034 of the waste storage permit for the interim radioactive waste storage facility in nowhere else but Gorleben.[110] Even if the site selection process was completed by 2031 at the latest, it is doubtful that a radioactive waste disposal facility could be built in such a short time. Already indications are that the time frame by 2031 is too short,[111] however, as it is unrealistic that the completion of the site selection process alone can be done by 2031.[112] This is because, among other things, it will take at least 15 years to conduct an underground survey of the selected site.[113] The 2031 date is also based on the length of licenses granted to operate interim radioactive waste storage facilities at nuclear power plants. The first such storage facility began operation in December 2002 (SZL Lingen). A 40-year permit to operate an interim radioactive waste storage facility at a nuclear power plant site means a reserve of only 11 years in the event of a possible delay in selecting a site for the waste disposal facility. This is also the time for its construction and production launch. In addition, interim storage sites were created temporarily so that they could be emptied as quickly as possible, and their contents transported to a disposal facility. From the explanatory memorandum to the Act, it appears that such a time frame derives from the desire to ensure that the problem of selecting a site for a radioactive waste disposal facility is completed while "this generation" is still alive.[114]

Such a time frame shows a deliberate stretching of the very procedure of selecting the location of the final disposal facility. This will undoubtedly require time so that appropriate studies of each potential site can be conducted. In addition, stretching the process out until 2031 disconnects the choice of disposal facility location from the election cycle. This will undoubtedly promote the development of a compromise. The process itself will be handled by politicians, civil servants, and all other stakeholders who are not of one generation. They will represent at least three generations, which increases the chance of developing a lasting cross-generational compromise. As an example of how solutions have been worked out over a long period of time, protests over the decision to create Gorleben facility have been ongoing since the beginning of the construction of this radioactive waste disposal facility in the 1980s. Binding arrangements were not made until *Atomausstieg I* and then *Atomausstieg II*.

The danger of such a drawn-out way of working out solutions is that a resolution may ultimately not be reached at all. Over such a long period of time (i.e. until 2031), such a large number of scientific, political, economic, legal, or social arguments can be formulated both for and against each possible location that it may lead to complete decision paralysis.[115] Stretching the decision-making process out over time like this – until 2031 – could also cause the process of selecting a disposal site to lose the necessary momentum, or that it would be aborted or abandoned altogether. In the future, the social situation may change and the problem of radioactive waste management and disposal will lose its social importance, although the problem itself will not disappear. The downside to the solution of stretching out the process of selecting a final disposal facility is that a decision will not be made when there is the most public support to resolve this issue, which is right now.

5. Commission for high-level radioactive waste disposal as an institutional novelty

The 2013-*Standortauswahlgesetz* stipulates that the selection of the location of a radioactive waste disposal facility will be preceded by the work of a commission that is established by the Act itself. Pursuant to §3(1), sentence 1 of 2013-*Standortauswahlgesetz*, a High-Level Radioactive Waste Disposal Commission was established (*Kommission Lagerung hoch radioaktiver Abfallstoffe*; further: HLRWD-Commission). The Commission's work period was 2014–2016. The Commission's task, according to 2013-*Standortauswahlgesetz*, was to first develop a technical and organisational framework in the political process[116] and then to carry out the actual selection process for the location of the radioactive waste disposal facility.[117] The status of this body derives from §3(1) *in fine*, according to which the Commission is established within the respective committee of the Bundestag. The administrative services of the Commission shall be provided by the Chancellery of the Bundestag.

HLRWD-Commission consisted of 32 members. HLRWD-Commission can be described as "hybrid state institution"[118] because of its composition. It consisted of eight representatives of science, two representatives of environmental organisations, two representatives of churches or other religious organisations, two representatives of economy (economic organisations), and two representatives of trade unions. The indicated members, in accordance with §3(1), sentence 3 of *Standortauswahlgesetz*, were elected by the Bundestag and the Bundesrat on the basis of a joint proposal from the parliamentary groups for all candidates. The Commission also included eight members of the Bundestag, representing all parliamentary factions, as well as eight representatives of Länder governments.

The composition of HLRWD-Commission was deliberately chosen by the lawmaker.[119] Four different groups with eight members each represent different social groups: representatives of the social partners, representatives of science, members of the Bundestag and representatives of the Länder. This composition of the Commission was presumably intended to enable it to achieve its statutory objective of working out a compromise between state and society, between the Federation and the Länder, and between the citizens themselves.

Representatives of society and representatives of science were elected by members of the Bundestag. This may raise questions as to whether it is certain that the individuals selected by the MPs adequately represent the public side and science, if, for example, they are not local leaders or chairs of relevant scientific committees. The involvement of the Bundestag in the election of the representatives of society and science is stipulated by Article 20(2) of the Basic Law. In the case of authorities that do not come directly from direct elections, it is required that there is a so-called chain of legitimacy *(Legitimationskette)*.[120] Indeed, the exercise of public power requires such democratic legitimacy.[121] The FCC in 1978 indicated that the constitutional principle of democracy extends to all possible forms of exercise of state power.[122] Subsequently, it was further clarified that this applies to any official action related to making a sovereign decision.[123] This is because such sovereign decisions are an exercise of state power, so it must be possible to show that they originate with the People.[124] Hence, both the organs of state power, their composition and the actions taken by them should have a basis in the settlement of the People.[125] This means that there must be an unbroken chain of democratic legitimacy for either the body in question or for specific decisions of public authority.[126] Only when there is such a chain of legitimacy is it possible to fulfil the constitutional injunction that all state power must come from the People.[127]

A quarter of the Commission consisted of members who were directly elected by the German people in elections (Bundestag deputies). The status of state representatives varies quite a bit. Some of the members from the Länder were directly elected members of local parliaments (F. Untersteller, U. Scharf, C. Pegel, S. Wenzel, T. Schmidt, R. Habeck). All of these individuals were also ministers in their respective state governments.[128] Some representatives of the Länder in turn served then as ministers in Land governments (G. Duin, C. Dalbert). In this case, the chain of legitimacy is longer, as the election of the state government by the local (national) parliament (elected in a Land) must be taken into account. The same status applies to all Länder representatives who are alternates to current commission members.[129] In the case of the 16 representatives of society and science, their legitimacy lies in the fact that they were elected by the Bundestag. Of particular interest is the involvement of representatives of religious associations. This follows a tradition of Evangelical Church representatives getting involved on the side of those protesting against nuclear power.[130]

An equal number of permanent substitutes were appointed for MPs and Länder representatives. The automatic appointment of deputies is a parliamentary custom in Germany, unknown, for example, in the Polish parliamentary tradition. The application of this practice also for HLRWD-Commission underlines its importance. The reason for this is that twice as many representatives of the Bundestag and of the Länder were involved in the matter – the appointed deputies must be kept abreast of the state of the HLRWD-Commission's work in order to be able to act as deputies at any time. This custom also improved the efficiency of the HLRWD-Commission, as it ensured continuity in its operations and prevents its work from being interrupted due to insufficient members. On the other hand, it is negative that the appointment of deputies did not apply to the social and scientific side (i.e. representatives of science, environmental organisations, religious associations, the economy and trade unions). The representation of the political side (i.e. the Bundestag and Länder governments) was institutionally ensured to be complete. Unfortunately, in the case of the social side and scientific representatives, they will not always be fully represented, if only in the event of absence for cause. In practice, however, a problem could arise in the form of having to clearly identify a primary person (i.e. a permanent member of the Commission) and a secondary person (i.e. an alternate). In constitutional terms, election by the Bundestag would also have to include deputies to ensure the principle of chain of legitimacy.

The legal status of the HLRWD-Commission's members representing the public and science is also different. Only representatives of society and science were given the right to vote on the final report (as opposed to members of the Bundestag and representatives of the Länder). This formation of the composition of the HLRWD-Commission was a direct consequence of the intention to achieve the widest possible consensus within 2013-*Standortauswahlgesetz*, not only among the political forces but also in society as a whole.[131] It appears that giving only social and scientific members of the Commission a vote on the final report may have been an effective attempt to bridge the divisions in society and the rift that occurred between the public and political forces over the nuclear waste issue. By giving the public side and representatives of science a say in the final form of the report, they will not be able to evade responsibility in the future as to the theses contained in the final report of the HLRWD-Commission's work. An example of this attitude can be seen in the frontal criticism of any outcome of the HLRWD-Commission's work related to the selection of a site for a radioactive waste disposal facility. The decisive voice of the social side means that by engaging in the work of the HLRWD-Commission, it took co-responsibility for the solutions worked out. In turn, the representatives of the Bundestag who have been involved in the work of the HLRWD-Commission at all times will not be able to disregard the HLRWD-Commission's findings either. In fact, this applies to the entire Bundestag, since Members of Parliament represent their parliamentary clubs when they work in the Commission. Thus, the engagement mechanism provided by the Act is a thoughtful solution that provided an opportunity to develop appropriate outcomes, i.e. compromise between the various parties to the dispute.

The main task of the Commission, according to §3(2) of 2013-*Standortauswahlgesetz*, was to prepare a report. The report, as provided in §4(1), should prepare the process for the disposal facility site selection. The report was to include a discussion and evaluation of issues relevant to neutralisation of radioactive waste. An important part of the report was to be the recommendations for future action that will be formulated by the HLRWD-Commission on the basis of the material collected. The recommendations of the Commission were then to be presented to the Bundestag and the Bundesrat. The HLRWD-Commission's report should also, pursuant to §4(1) *in fine* of the Act, analyse the experience and activities of other states on the issue of disposal facility selection.

The scope of the HLRWD-Commission was very clearly outlined in §3(4) of 2013-*Standortauswahlgesetz*. According to this provision, the HLRWD-Commission may, within the scope of its tasks, also take a position on the decisions already made (by the legislature) and the findings to date on the choice of the location for the radioactive waste disposal facility. Thus, the scope of the HLRWD-Commission is not just about the future. This is because it can express itself on matters that have already been raised in public debate and have been the subject of decisions by public authorities. Reference is made to §3(3) of 2013-*Standortauswahlgesetz* which gives HLRWD-Commission the right to submit drafts of the new wording of provisions of the Act to Bundestag. However, they will not be binding on the Bundestag.

§4(5) of 2013-*Standortauswahlgesetz* grants HLRWD-Commission even broader powers. Under this provision, the exemptions, minimum standards, and other bases developed by the HLRWD-Commission for deciding on the location and technical conditions for a high-level radioactive waste disposal facility are to be presented as recommendations and may then be adopted by the Bundestag in the form of a law. This wording of §4(5) of 2013-*Standortauswahlgesetz* may come as a surprise. The explanatory memorandum points out that the HLRWD-Commission's recommendations are only of a technical and scientific nature and represent the voice of society on the content of the new federal law and will not be binding on the Bundestag.[132] Putting these recommendations into statutory form, however, may have a different effect. Two options are possible: the recommendations of HLRWD-Commission will be included in the articulated portion of the bill; the recommendations of the HLRWD-Commission will be included and introduced as an appendix to the bill. Each of these provisions of the Act is prescriptive in nature. The adoption of these recommendations in statutory form will be binding on the Bundestag. The Bundestag shall remain bound until such time as it has either enacted a different law, or repealed it or the relevant part thereof. For the executive and judicial branches, however, the law (and the HLRWD-Commission's recommendations contained therein) will be fully binding until it is fully or partially derogated from by the Bundestag. Due to the hierarchy of sources of law, the recommendations formulated in a federal law will be binding on the authorities of the constituent states of the Federation.

Legislating in the manner envisaged for the HLRWD-Commission by 2013-*Standortauswahlgesetz*, is undoubtedly technocratic in nature. This is because the content of the bill is developed by a team of experts together with parliamentarians (not all stakeholder groups). Missing from this body are representatives of energy companies, i.e. those entities that are responsible for the generation of radioactive waste. This is most likely due to the fact that the general German public has a distrust of lobbying by these corporations. Most likely, the authors of 2013-*Standortauswahlgesetz* wanted to avoid accusations that there was a "covenant democracy" in the case of radioactive waste as well,[133] as *Atomausstieg I*, *Laufzeitverlängerung* and *Atomausstieg II* were viewed.[134] In this case, a paradoxical situation has arisen: the law is created with reference to a specific group of entities, namely nuclear power companies, and the consequences of their actions (the radioactive waste they produce) without their participation at all. Such a move by the legislature could be seen as rebuking them by taking away the right of responsible energy companies to participate in the process. This can also be interpreted to mean that in the nearly 60 years since Germany entered nuclear power, the German nuclear industry has not developed appropriate solutions for the disposal of radioactive waste. So since the nuclear industry had failed to ensure this, it was necessary for the rest to carry it out. Yet another explanation for the legislature's action may have to do with the fact that, until now, energy companies have accumulated considerable expertise and experience in waste issues. On the other hand, representatives of individual representative groups (policy makers, scientific representatives, environmental organisations, trade unions, religious associations and churches) had smaller and rather dispersed knowledge. The possibility of joint work in the HLRWD-Commission, and thus the accumulation of knowledge by representatives of these groups may be a procedure that will balance the current disproportion in knowledge resources. However, the condition should be met that the process of acquiring this knowledge is not distorted by entities with a sufficiently large pool of knowledge, i.e. energy companies. However, the explanatory memorandum to the bill does not provide any explanation for the solution adopted to exclude energy companies from the Commission's work.

2013-*Standortauswahlgesetz* has not determined whether comments can be made on the text of such a bill as it moves through the Bundestag. From the lack of regulation on this matter, it should be inferred that such a possibility is not envisaged and parliamentarians will immediately vote on the finished draft text of the law. Solutions, as to the preparation of ready-made drafts of EU legislation, are applied in EU legislation. This applies, for example, to EU regulations, which then have the character of general law, on which parliamentarians vote in full for or against. The solution in the 2013-*Standortauswahlgesetz* is not as technocratic as it might initially seem, since half of the Commission is made up of parliamentarians. However, this formulation of the provisions of *Standortauswahlgesetz* appears to be a deliberate effort: HLRWD-Commission is to be the body that plays a pivotal role in the process of selecting a disposal facility site.

The law clearly identified areas for which the HLRWD-Commission was to develop recommendations in its report. In the first instance, according to §4(2)(1) of 2013-*Standortauswahlgesetz*, HLRWD-Commission is to examine whether, instead of the imminent disposal of highly radioactive waste in deep geological layers, other possibilities for the orderly disposal of this waste should not be scientifically investigated. At the same time, radioactive waste would continue to be housed in interim radioactive waste storage facilities until testing is completed.

The next task for the HLRWD-Commission was to ensure that the report is a suitable basis for the Bundestag to decide on specific issues. In accordance with §4(2)(2) of 2013-*Standortauswahlgesetz*, the catalogue of these matters included: general safety requirements for the storage of radioactive waste criteria for the exclusion of specific locations with reference to geology, water management and zoning; minimum requirements for individual geological formations for a disposal facility, including criteria for the selection and possible exclusion of rock salt, marble and crystal deposits, as well as criteria independent of the selected geological formations; methodology for conducting future safety studies. An important element of the bill will be the administration of so-called stress-tests.[135] The safety tests will simulate various scenarios of special stress on the final disposal facility. This will help establish the resilience of the location data of a future final disposal facility in the event that extreme adverse scenarios materialise.

The third area developed in HLRWD-Commission's report was to be the criteria for making possible adjustments in the ongoing location proceedings (§4(2)(3) of 2013-*Standortauswahlgesetz*). It is a question of formulating requirements for the disposal concept, especially with regard to the possibility of bringing the stored radioactive waste back to the surface. It should be pointed out that the feasibility of bringing waste back to the surface generally depends on the type of geological strata selected for the landfill.[136]

The fourth topic area of the report, according to §4(2)(4) of 2013-*Standortauswahlgesetz*, was to be the criteria for organising and carrying out the process of selecting the disposal site and checking other possible sites.

The fifth and final topic area was to be the criteria for public involvement and access to information to ensure transparency in the site selection process.

Finally, the legislature indicated that the report should also discuss the socio-political aspects of the process of selecting the location of the waste disposal facility, in addition to any relevant issues of a technical and scientific nature.

The HLRWD-Commission's report was to be divided into two parts: "organizing the selection process" and "technical part".[137] On one hand the first part served to make recommendations to the Bundestag on how to proceed with the site selection process and to conduct an evaluation of 2013-*Standortauswahlgesetz* itself.[138] On the other hand, the HLRWD-Commission had to create opportunities for public participation within selection process.[139] The technical part was to have *de facto* legal force with respect to technical requirements, and their criteria will be enacted directly by the Bundestag.[140] §3(5), sentence 1 of the 2013-*Standortauswahlgesetz* provided that the report should be adopted unanimously. If this fails, then the report may be adopted by a two-thirds majority of the statutory number of members of the HLRWD-Commission. Each member of the HLRWD-Commission shall have the right to present a dissenting opinion, which must be attached to the report as an integral part thereof.

The Act set a deadline for the HLRWD-Commission to prepare the report by 31 December 2015 (§3(5) of 2013-*Standortauswahlgesetz*). The Act provided for a one-time extension of six months. This deadline was not met as the report was presented beyond the deadline.

Already in 2014 it was questioned whether the Commission will achieve its stated goal of consensus building.[141] Neither the composition of the Commission as presented nor the solutions worked out by it guaranteed the achievement of the intended purpose.[142] The Bundestag at the end of this procedure was not constrained by any solutions, and those adopted by the Bundestag might differ from the results of the Commission's work, as well as from the results of the public consultation.[143] However, this scenario did not materialise because Bundestag followed HLRWD-Commission's recommendations.

6. Elements of transparency pursuant to *Standortauswahlgesetz*

The explanatory memorandum to 2013-*Standortauswahlgesetz* made it very clear that HLRWD-Commission was established to ensure the transparency of the proceedings as a whole, as well as to develop recommendations for the evaluation of the 2013-*Standortauswahlgesetz*.[144] This is important because §1(2) of 2013-*Standortauswahlgesetz* provides that as long as the Commission is still working (it is not a matter of evaluating the Act itself), the procedure for selecting a site for the radioactive waste disposal facility cannot be initiated. The adoption of the report in accordance with §5(4) shall take place at the last meeting of HLRWD-Commission, which also terminates its work.

Transparency of the Commission's work was to be ensured by the public nature of its meetings. §5(1), sentence 2 of 2013-*Standortauswahlgesetz* provided for the possibility of live streaming Commission meetings on the Internet. Meeting minutes, commissioned technical opinions and analyses and the final report were also public.

The first institutional solution to strengthen the transparency of the process was the establishment of the National Civil Society Board (*Gesellschaftliches Begleitgremium*[145]/*Nationales Begleitgremium*).[146] According to §8 of 2013-*Standortauswahlgesetz*, after HLRWD-Commission has completed its work, the Federal Ministry for the Environment and Reactor Safety is to appoint, with the approval of the Bundestag and Bundesrat, a National Civil Society Board. The purpose of the Council is to be concerned with the common good while accompanying the progress of selecting the site for the radioactive waste disposal facility. Pursuant to §8 of 2013- and 2017-*Standortauswahlgesetz*, the members of the Board are to be granted access to all relevant documents of all entities involved into the selection procedure. The positions and guidelines developed by the Board are to be published. At the same time, dissenting opinions submitted by individual members of the Board are to be recorded.

The 2013-*Standortauswahlgesetz* lacked provisions regarding the National Civil Society Board, so it was difficult to assess back in 2013 the composition of this body. Since the work of the Board has been scheduled after the HLRWD-Commission finished its work, it was reasonable to assume that, in all likelihood, some of the members of HLRWD-Commission might become part of the newly appointed Board. This would be a natural continuation of the HLRWD-Commission's work. Existing Commission members would be given the opportunity to review on an ongoing basis how the HLRWD-Commission's recommendations are being implemented. The 2013-*Standortauswahlgesetz* lacked a provision allowing HLRWD-Commission members to join the Board. However, due to the plurality of views presented, it would also be important to expand the Council to include other members. Those assumptions materialised because indeed some of HLRWD-Commission did join the Board.[147]

7. Final site selection in the form of enactment of a federal law dedicated to the issue

The procedure for selecting the final location of the radioactive waste disposal facility involves five steps (modified already in 2017 – so even before the selection process started for good). The first stage involved the already discussed proceedings as part of the action of the HLRWD-Commission, which resulted in publication of the report in 2016.[148] The results of the Commission's work were to involve identifying the regions and developing conditions and criteria. Further work, on the basis of those findings, is to be undertaken by BGE (*Bundesgesellschaft für Endlagerung*), a newly established company owned solely by the Federal Republic of Germany.[149] The possibility of privatising public tasks by transferring them to a private law entity is excluded thanks to this manoeuvre. BGE became the operator of existing repositories of non-high-level radioactive waste (Konrad and Morsleben) and within selection process is responsible for searching site for the final repository and for submitting proposals to the Federal Government.[150] Its work is supervised by the newly established supervisory authority: Federal Office for the Safety of Nuclear Waste Management (*Bundesamt für die Sicherheit der nuklearen Entsorgung*, further: BASE). Main task of BASE is licensing and supervision of nuclear fuel transport, radioactive waste interim storage and site selection process.[151] Another task of this new authority is organisation of public participation within the site selection process.[152] Although BASE was formed on the basis of restructuring of other federal agencies and authorities, it is a genuine new institution as it gained new legal responsibilities.[153] The Federal Ministry for the Environment and Reactor Safety (BMU), which supervises both BGE and

BASE, is also an important player within selection proceedings.[154] Each successive stage of *Standortauswahlgesetz* is to culminate in the adoption of a law by the Bundestag, the content of which will consist of the results of the work of that stage.

The second stage will be conducted by BGE as the project developer. §13 of *Standortauswahlgesetz* requires BGE to examine the locations on the basis of the safety criteria set by this Federal Act, taking into account the public interest. This phase, in accordance with §13(2) of the Act, is to be semi-concluded with the operator publishing as well as submitting to BASE a report on the criteria for exclusion and on areas that seem to be particularly convenient. Basing on this report, BGE is – according to §14 – expected to submit its proposal of areas for further ground surveys (along with results of public participation).

The third stage is the revision by BASE of the area proposals. The supervisory authority may, after verification, either confirm BGE's choice of location or make a different choice (§15(1), sentence 2). Subsequently, BASE is to submit a report to BMU with proposals for areas for ground survey, including results of public participation, recommendations from the National Civil Society Board and its own recommendation with appropriate justification (§15(2), sentence 1). Finally, the Federal Government is to inform the Bundestag of the areas which should be selected for further work (§15(2), sentence 2). According to §15(3) of *Standortauswahlgesetz*, Bundestag decides in statutory form on areas designated for further above-ground survey work.

The fourth stage consists of several phases. The project developer should undertake at first reconnaissance works and on their basis develop programme of safety measures. Simultaneously BGE should also develop a socio-economic analysis of potential of every area (§16(1)). BGE should then develop specific criteria on the basis of initial findings that will enable undertaking underground works as well as criteria for excluding particular areas. In the end, BGE along with those developed criteria sends to BASE its proposal of areas where underground works should be undertaken.

The fifth step involves a review by the supervisory authority (BASE) of the conclusions and areas recommended by BGE. Similarly to third stage, BASE verifies proposal of BGE and may not support it and change it. BASE is to then submit a report to BMU with proposals for areas for underground survey, including results of public participation, recommendations from the National Civil Society Board and its own recommendation with appropriate justification. Finally, the Federal Government is to inform the Bundestag of the areas which should be selected for further work (§17(2), sentence 3). According to §17(2) sentence 4 of *Standortauswahlgesetz*, Bundestag decides in statutory form on areas designated for further underground survey work.

Within the sixth step, BGE is required to implement its plan of underground work (§18(1)). The project developer also prepares the documentation necessary to conduct an environmental impact assessment of the considered locations for the disposal facility.

The seventh step is that BGE informs BASE about the location for the disposal facility that it recommends. This recommendation should contain results of the comparison of potential locations that BGE assessed on the basis of criteria previously developed and approved by BASE. It is BASE that then conducts the environmental impact assessment of the location that BGE recommended. What distinguishes this stage from the previous ones is the fact that this time the supervisory authority (BASE) makes its own decision in regards to the location (and does not only supervise and forward decisions undertaken by BGE as in earlier phases). Thus BASE on the basis of §19(2) of *Standortauswahlgesetz* presents to BMU a site proposal with all necessary documents. This stage included both public participation as well as judicial review.

The final, eighth step is for the Bundestag and Bundesrat to decide on the final location of the high-level radioactive waste final disposal facility in the form of a law. Before this can happen, however, BMU is required to verify that the selection of the final site has been carried out in accordance with the requirements stipulated by *Standortauswahlgesetz*. If the results of this analysis are positive, the Federal Government shall submit a location proposal to the Bundestag in the form of a law. The Bundestag, pursuant to §20(2) of *Standortauswahlgesetz*. At the same time, under §20(3) of *Standortauswahlgesetz*, the final (statutory) decision on the selection of the final disposal facility location is binding in the administrative proceedings under Atomic Law on the granting of a license to operate such an installation (i.e. final disposal facility).

8. Way forward

It is worth contrasting the statutory assumptions with the reality resulting from the final report of the Commission established by the *Standortauswahlgesetz*. On 5 July 2016, the Commission completed its nearly 700-page report of nearly two years of work.[155] The most important problem identified in the report appeared to be the postponement by several decades of the timetable for the creation of a disposal facility for radioactive waste – perhaps even into the 22nd century(!). It has also become clear that a disposal facility will not be built until the licenses to operate interim radioactive waste storage facilities located at nuclear power plants expire.[156] The timetable adopted in 2013- and 2017-*Standortauswahlgesetz* which stipulated that a decision on the location of the disposal facility would be made around 2031 and that it would begin operation, as estimated, around 2050, was determined by policy-makers solely on the basis of the length of permits to operate interim radioactive waste storages.[157] An unambiguous message was presented in the Bundestag press release on the work of the HLRWD-Commission,[158] published even before the end of its work. HLRWD-Commission did not depart from the statutory timetable (which provides for a site determination in 2031), but instead provided the earliest date for the high-level radioactive waste final disposal facility determination in 2048.[159] The HLRWD-Commission also did not rule out the start of the radioactive waste disposal facility until the next century,[160] i.e. the 22nd century. The final report merely points out that subsequent implementation phases may take longer, as the time required to complete them is not easy to estimate. Of course, it is impossible to say that the HLRWD-Commission is to blame for the delay. The HLRWD-Commission merely updated the work schedule, and this was undoubtedly the main message from the HLRWD-Commission's work even before it was completed.[161] This approach may be due to a different ordering of priorities related to the disposal of radioactive waste than one might think. While the HLRWD-Commission's position is that it is important to dispose of radioactive waste without disrupting schedules, safety and public participation are priorities in this task.[162] This means that the realisation of the high-level radioactive waste final disposal facility is not an end in itself. With that in mind, it is worth examining the rest of the HLRWD-Commission's report as well.

It is important to note the conclusions that emerge from the final report regarding the process to select the location and technology for the radioactive waste disposal facility. The most important seems to be the introduction of the principle of reversibility of any decision made during these proceedings.[163] This is because the HLRWD-Commission wants to leave open the possibility of correcting decisions that turn out to be wrong in the future due to unforeseeable circumstances.[164] This approach is based on introduction into site selection procedure of an "error culture".[165] Reversibility of decisions is also supposed to be based on ethical considerations – the idea is to leave the possibility for future generations to make their own decisions (e.g. by changing the existing arrangements).[166] The HLRWD-Commission indicates that following the principle of reversibility is intended to provide greater confidence in the process of selecting a disposal facility for radioactive waste.[167] While the HLRWD-Commission has stipulated that unnecessary reversals of determinations made should be avoided,[168] there is no way to make this recommendation a reality. While it appears that reversibility may increase public acceptance of the process of selecting a disposal facility, it entails the risk of creating further delays or even disrupting the decision cycle. This is confirmed by the HLRWD-Commission itself, noting the possibility of a significant lengthening of subsequent stages over time.[169]

The HLRWD-Commission intends to apply the reversibility principle primarily to the concept of disposal itself. It is to be located in underground geological strata, as only there is passive safety guaranteed that will not require continuous maintenance.[170] These are findings mostly known even before the work on *Standortauswahlgesetz* began. In addition, the HLRWD-Commission recommends that an underground facility be equipped with a reversibility mechanism with the option to retrieve radioactive waste, in case the need arises, for example, from new knowledge.[171] The ability to retrieve radioactive waste is also to be ensured once the disposal facility is sealed, which will operate in a mode of operation that does not require ongoing maintenance.[172] This primarily involves the parallel existence of another high-level radioactive waste final disposal facility, ready to receive radioactive waste from the existing one[173] (so the waste containers will have to be retrievable).

The report devotes considerable length to issues of public information and transparency. In addition to what follows from *Standortauswahlgesetz*, it is worth pointing out that the HLRWD-Commission advocated that the composition of National Civil Society Board *(Nationales Begleitgremium*) that is to accompany the process of selecting the location of the radioactive waste disposal facility be expanded to eighteen members. Six persons were to be selected at random from this group, at least two of whom will represent the youngest generation (16–27 years of age), and 12 well-known persons from public life are to be identified by the Bundestag and Bundesrat.[174] The task of the Board is to identify the need for changes and possible innovations in relation to the adopted procedure and to propose them directly to the legislature.[175]

Hence, the solutions of *Standortauswahlgesetz* were subject to criticism even before they were presented in the HLRWD-Commission's report. It has been pointed out that the procedure based on the *Standortauswahlgesetz* is a unique combination of administrative procedure with public involvement and legislative procedure, but leads to a kind of overemphasis on the selection process and at the same time deprives the participatory elements of effectiveness.[176] It is therefore discouraged to replicate the model adopted in connection with the *Standortauswahlgesetz* in the event that other large infrastructure projects are implemented by public authorities.[177]

Another instrument proposed in the HLRWD-Commission's report is the development of agreements on a specific future location for the final disposal facility.[178] Such an agreement is not only intended to establish an equivalent to a region for placing a radioactive waste final disposal facility on its territory.[179] It is also intended to contain many of the basic elements about the future installation that will not be affected (such as access roads, surface area, protection from emissions, storage capacity, storage technology), as well as long-term commitments on how the installation will operate during its start-up period, as well as during the transition to the final stage – sealing of the final disposal facility.[180]

The Commission also evaluated the *Standortauswahlgesetz* itself, and made many recommendations to the legislature which were implemented through the 2017 Amendment. The Commission has asked the Federal Government to come up with an appropriate regulation as soon as possible in order to find a suitable solution for the protection of possible locations for the radioactive waste disposal facility.[181] In addition, the Commission has asked that the current consensus to ban the "export" of radioactive waste generated in commercial nuclear reactors also be extended to waste generated in research nuclear reactors.[182] The Commission also asked for a statutory general ban on the export of high-level radioactive waste.[183]

Finally, it is worth contrasting the content of the final report on the HLRWD-Commission's work with the critical voices expressed both in the dissenting opinions to the report, in the public debate, and in the literature on the subject. Although the Commission's work lasted nearly two years, it failed to initiate a broader public debate around the subject of *Standortauswahlgesetz*.[184] However, some of the Commission's work has received public backlash, most notably that concerning the update to the nuclear waste disposal schedule, which was accomplished by postponing by several decades the determination of the final location of the waste disposal facility and the associated start of the final disposal facility only in the 22nd century. The Commission had to accept that it had therefore insufficiently addressed the huge problem of continued above-ground storage of high-radioactive waste in interim radioactive waste storage facilities.[185] The problem of the safety of the population living in the vicinity of these dozens of interim radioactive waste storages will not be solved, and the final report itself omits this topic.[186]

Another concern arising from the Commission's report is the purpose of the radioactive waste disposal facility. The result of the Commission's work is the question of the type of radioactive waste for which a disposal facility is to be designed, and whether one facility is enough.[187] There is a whole group of intermediate radioactive wastes which are not amenable to disposal in a disposal facility for low and intermediate level waste, and it is not clear from the Commission's work whether the criteria for selecting a site for a high-level radioactive waste final disposal facility will include these intermediate radioactive wastes.[188]

An additional measure (that just recently popped up in the public debate) worth consideration within the site selection process is the voluntary siting approach.[189] Voluntarism is suggested to be included as one of criteria for the site selection process.[190] Taking into account this new approach also seems to be a good way forward.

Finally, there is no explicit demand in the HLRWD-Commission's report to amend the Grundgesetz and introduce provisions affirming the nuclear phase-out.[191] Although the HLRWD-Commission commissioned two legal studies on the subject,[192] it presented the settlement of this issue only as a possible action by the legislature.[193] However, taking into account the amount of activity undertaken by different state bodies, previous and current activity of civil society and the will to find a compromise within the society, amending *Grundgesetz* seems to be a good way forward.

Notes

1 Publ. BGBl. I, p. 1074 et seq.

2 See BVerfGE104,238, p. 239.

3 See further: A.Tiggemann, *The elephant in the room. The role of Gorleben and its site selection in the German nuclear waste debate* [in:] A.Brunnengräber, M.Di Nucci (eds.), *Conflicts, participation and acceptability in nuclear waste governance*, Wiesbaden 2019, p. 70. See also FCC judgment BVerfGE104,238, p. 240.

4 O.Däuper, K.Bosch, R.Ringwald, *Zur Finanzierung des Standortauswahlverfahrens für ein atomares Endlager durch Beiträge der Abfallverursacher*, "ZUR" 2013, p. 329; Bundesminister des Innern, *Antwort der Bundesregierung auf die Große Anfrage der Abgeordneten Dr. Laufs, Dr. Dregger, Spranger, Dr. Riesenhuber, Dr. Miltner, Lenzer, Broll, Fellner, Dr. von Geldern, Gerlach, Dr. Waffenschmidt, Dr. Bugl, Gerstein, Frau Hürland, Kolb, Dr. George, Dr. Jobst, Dr. Köhler (Wolfsburg), Dr. Kunz (Weiden), Magin, Pfeffermann, Prangenberg, Schwarz, Dr. Stavenhagen und der Fraktion der CDU/CSU – Drucksache 9/858 – Verantwortung des Bundes für Sicherstellung und Endlagerung radioaktiver Abfälle in der Bundesrepublik Deutschland* of 22 December 1981, „Deutscher Bundestag Drucksache 9/1231", pp. 1–7. For a detailed account of that "selection" process – see A.Tiggemann, *The elephant . . .* , pp. 71–74.

5 A.Tiggemann, *The elephant . . .* , p. 85; U.Wollenteit, *Gorleben und kein Ende*, "ZUR" 2014, p. 323.

6 J.Olliges *A "Deliberative Turn" in German Nuclear Waste Governance?* [in:] A.Brunnengräber, M.Di Nucci (eds.), *Conflicts . . .* , p. 262.

7 A.Losada, D.Themann, M.Di Nucci, *Experts and politics in the German nuclear waste governance* [in:] A.Brunnengräber, M.Di Nucci (eds.), *Conflicts . . .* , p. 240; A.Tiggemann, *The Elephant . . .* , p. 79; HLRWD-Commission, *Abschlussbericht. Verantwortung für die Zukunft. Ein faires und transparentes Verfahren für die Auswahl eines nationalen Endlagerstandortes*, Berlin 2016, p. 97.

8 Bundesminister des Innern, *Antwort . . .* , p. 2–3.

9 Ibid.

10 For reasons to choose salt as host rock: A.Tiggemann, *The elephant . . .* , pp. 71–72.

11 Bundesminister des Innern, *Antwort . . .* , p. 6.

12 Cf. BVerfGE104,238, p. 240.

13 A.Tiggemann, *The Elephant . . .* , pp. 72–74; HLRWD-Commission, *Abschlussbericht . . .* , p. 95; A.Tiggemann, *Gorleben – Entsorgungsstandort auf der*

Grundlage eines sachgerechten Auswahlverfahrens, "Atomwirtschaft" 2010, vol. 10, p. 606–611; Deutscher Depeschendienst, *Interview: Endlager Gorleben aus Expertensicht nur zweite Wahl.* <www.verivox.de/nachrichten/interview-endlager-gorleben-aus-expertensicht-nur-zweite-wahl-43384/>.

14 Deutscher Depeschendienst, *Interview . . .*

15 See A.Tiggemann, *Der niedersächsische Auswahl- und Entscheidungsprozess. Expertise zur Standortauswahl für das "Entsorgungszentrum" 1976/77*, Hannover 2010, p. 79. www.umwelt.niedersachsen.de/download/35842; Deutscher Depeschendienst, *Interview . . .*

16 A.Losada, D.Themann, M.Di Nucci, *Experts . . .*, p. 240.

17 A.Tiggemann, *Der niedersächsische . . .*, p. 79; Deutscher Depeschendienst, *Interview . . .*

18 A.Kirchhof, H.Trischler, *The history behind West Germany's nuclear phase-out* [in:] A.Kirchhof (ed.), *Pathways into and out of nuclear power in Western Europe Austria, Denmark, Federal Republic of Germany, Italy, and Sweden*, Munich 2020, p. 152.

19 A.Tiggemann, *Der niedersächsische . . .*, p. 80–81.

20 A.Tiggemann, *Gorleben . . .*, p. 610.

21 See further J.Kamlage, J.Warode, A.Mengede, *Chances, challenges and choices of participation in siting a nuclear waste repository* [in:] A.Brunnengräber, M.Di Nucci (eds.), *Conflicts . . .*, p. 93–94.

22 U.Wollenteit, *Gorleben . . .*, p. 324.

23 A.Tiggemann, *The elephant . . .*, p. 70.

24 O.Däuper, K.Bosch, R.Ringwald, *Zur Finanzierung . . .*, p. 329.

25 Own translation based on the contract available in: P.Becker, *Aufstieg und Krise der deutschen Stromkonzerne*, Bochum 2011, p. 353.

26 The text of the statement is presented in Appendix 1.

27 As stated in FCC judgment BVerfGE104,238, p. 241.

28 See FCC judgement of 5 December 2001, ref. 2 BvG 1/00, publ. BVerfGE104,238. This ruling is commonly referred to as: Moratorium Gorleben.

29 BVerfGE104,238, p. 239.

30 Ibid.

31 Published in "Bulletin der Bundesregierung", 11 October 1979, no. 122, p. 1133.

32 A.Tiggemann, *The elephant . . .*, p. 72.

33 BVerfGE104,238, p. 242.

34 Ibid.

35 Ibid., p. 243.

36 Ibid.

37 Ibid., pp. 243–244.

38 Ibid., p. 244.

39 Ibid.

40 Ibid.

41 Ibid.

42 Ibid., p. 245.

43 Ibid.

44 Ibid., p. 247.

45 Ibid., p. 249.

46 Ibid., p. 248.

47 Ibid., p. 249.

48 Ibid.

49 O.Däuper, K.Bosch, R.Ringwald, *Zur Finanzierung . . .*, p. 329.

50 Ibid.
51 Ibid.; and P.Becker, *Aufstieg . . .* , p. 212.
52 K.Röhlig, *The ENTRIA Project (2013–2018)* [in:] A.Brunnengräber, M.Di Nucci (eds.), *Conflicts . . .* , p. 317.
53 M.Schreurs, J.Suckow, *Bringing transparency and voice into the search for a deep geological repository. Nuclear waste governance in Germany and the role of the National Civil Society Board – Nationales Begleitgremium (NBG)* [in:] A.Brunnengräber, M.Di Nucci (eds.), *Conflicts . . .* , p. 296. However, the second more pragmatic reason was the need to implement Council Directive 2011/70/ Euratom of 19 July 2011 establishing a Community framework for the responsible and safe management of spent fuel and radioactive waste – see J.Olliges, *A "Deliberative . . .* , p. 264.
54 O.Däuper, K.Bosch, R.Ringwald, *Zur Finanzierung . . .* , p. 329.
55 As stated in explanatory memorandum to the bill, p. 34. But 2013 *Standortauswahlgesetz* based immensely on the previous work in 2000s – see A.Tiggemann, *The elephant . . .* , p. 78–81.
56 U.Wollenteit, *Gorleben . . .* , p. 323.
57 As stated in explanatory memorandum to the Act, p. 29.
58 A.Blowers, *The legacy of nuclear power and what should be done about it* [in:] A.Brunnengräber, M.Di Nucci (eds.), *Conflicts . . .* , p. 67. Similarly A.Losada, D.Themann, M.Di Nucci, *Experts . . .* , p. 256–257; C.Drögemüller, *Schlüsselakteure . . .* , p. 5.
59 Six years later, the compromise around the search process is not only about obtaining acceptance, but at least tolerance for the disposal facility – see J.Kamlage, J.Warode, A.Mengede, *Chances . . .* , p. 96.
60 Explanatory memorandum to the Act, p. 29.
61 Similarly M.Ramana, *Why technical solutions are insufficient. The abiding conundrum of nuclear waste* [in:] A.Brunnengräber, M.Di Nucci (eds.), *Conflicts . . .* , p. 29.
62 On risks and burdens see further J.Kamlage, J.Warode, A.Mengede, *Chances . . .* , pp. 95–96.
63 As stated in E.Bohne, M.Speyer, *Staat und Konfliktbewältigung bei Zukunftstechnologien*, „NVwZ" 1999, p. 1.
64 J.Kamlage, J.Warode, A.Mengede, *Chances . . .* , p. 102.
65 See inter alia FCC judgment of 17 December 2013, ref. 1 BvR 3139/08, 1 BvR 3386/08, section 162. See further R.Rybski, *Judgment of the Federal Constitutional Court of 17 December 2013. (ref: 1 BvR 3139/08, 1 BvR 3386/08) on energy security as a premise allowing expropriation for the purpose of constructing an open-pit lignite mine, "Przegląd Sejmowy" 2015, no. 5.*
66 J.Kamlage, J.Warode, A.Mengede, *Chances . . .* , p. 105; U.Wollenteit, *Gorleben . . .* , p. 324.
67 A.Tiggemann, *The elephant . . .* , p. 81.
68 See explanatory memorandum to the bill, p. 68.
69 P.Hocke, A.Brunnengräber, *Multi-level governance of nuclear waste disposal* [in:] A.Brunnengräber, M.Di Nucci (eds.), *Conflicts . . .* , p. 388–389; U.Wollenteit, *Gorleben. . .* , p. 323.
70 O.Däuper, K.Bosch, R.Ringwald, *Zur Finanzierung . . .* , p. 329.
71 M.Schreurs, J.Suckow, *Bringing transparency . . .* , p. 305. Already state of Bavaria attempted to overcome this approach – see further M.Schreurs, J.Suckow, *Bringing transparency . . .* , p. 306.
72 A.Tiggemann, *The elephant . . .* , pp. 82–83 and 85.

73 D.Häfner, *The future is still unwritten – history too. Overcoming the conflicts of the past in Germany* [in:] A.Brunnengräber, M.Di Nucci (eds.), *Conflicts . . .* , pp. 42–43 and 46–51. However, other suggest that this work has been already done by HLRWD-Commission: C.Drögemüller, *Schlüsselakteure der Endlager-Governance. Entsorgungsoptionen und – strategien radioaktiver Abfälle aus Sicht regionaler Akteure*, Wiesbaden 2018, p. 244.
74 HLRWD-Commission, *Abschlussbericht . . .* , p. 493.
75 Ibid., p. 493 and 501.
76 Ibid., p. 501 and 512.
77 H.Koch, A.Roβnagel, *Neue Energiepolitik und Ausstieg aus der Kernenergie*, "NVwZ" 2000, p. 9; A.Tiggemann, *The elephant . . .* , p. 79.
78 H.Koch, A.Roβnagel, *Neue Energiepolitik . . .* , p. 9.
79 §21b(4) provides: "Fees or benefits collected to date, to the extent that they have been collected to cover the costs incurred, shall not be refunded if the Federation system referred to in §9a(3) is not finally erected or permitted to be used [. . .]" (own translation).
80 H.Koch, A.Roβnagel, *Neue Energiepolitik . . .* , p. 9.
81 Based on the text of the contract available in: P.Becker, *Aufstieg . . .* , p. 353.
82 Ibid.
83 Ibid.
84 Ibid.
85 See explanatory memorandum to the bill, p. 29.
86 Ibid., p. 4.
87 Ibid., p. 5.
88 H.Koch, A.Roβnagel, *Neue Energiepolitik . . .* , p. 9.
89 Ibid.
90 See BMU press release No. 238/21 of 17.09.2021 "Bergwerk Gorleben wird geschlossen". <www.bmu.de/pressemitteilung/bergwerk-gorleben-wird-geschlossen>.
91 See explanatory memorandum to the bill, p. 2.
92 Ibid.
93 As stated in the explanatory memorandum to the Act, p. 30.
94 Ibid.
95 Ibid.
96 Publ. BGBl. 1997 II, p. 131.
97 See explanatory memorandum to the bill, p. 30.
98 Ibid.
99 Ibid., p. 2.
100 Bundesminister des Innern, *Antwort . . .* , p. 2 and 3; U.Wollenteit, *Gorleben . . .* , p. 323.
101 See explanatory memorandum to the bill, p. 2.
102 J.Niewodniczański, *Wprowadzenie do energetyki jądrowej* [in:] K.Jeleń, Z.Rau (eds.), *Energetyka jądrowa w Polsce*, Warszawa 2012, p. 40.
103 A.Brunnengräber, *The wicked problem of long term radioactive waste governance* [in:] A.Brunnengräber, M.Di Nucci (eds.), *Conflicts . . .* , p. 344.
104 H.Koch, A.Roβnagel, *Neuę Energiepolitik . . .* , p. 8.
105 Ibid.
106 Official Journal of the EU of 17 December 2010 series L item 334, pp. 17–119.
107 A.Brunnengräber, *The wicked problem . . .* , p. 343.
108 C.Drögemüller, *Schlüsselakteure . . .* , p. 4.

109 See explanatory memorandum to the bill, p. 2.
110 O.Däuper, A.Bernstorff, *Gesetz zur Suche und Auswahl eines Standortes für die Endlagerung radioaktiver Abfälle – zugleich ein Vorschlag für die Agenda der „Kommission Lagerung hoch radioaktiver Abfallstoffe"*, „ZUR" 2014, p. 25.
111 M.Schreurs, J.Suckow, *Bringing transparency*. . . , p. 300.
112 O.Däuper, A.Bernstorff, *Gesetz* . . . , p. 25.
113 Ibid.
114 As stated in the explanatory memorandum to the Act, p. 42.
115 Recent literature is beginning to see the materialisation of this risk. See eg. P.Hocke, A.Brunnengräber, *Multi-level governance* . . . , pp. 389–390.
116 For an assessment of that task see: J.Olliges, *A "Deliberative* . . . , pp. 269–286.
117 M.Wiegand, *Konsens durch Verfahren? Öffentlichkeitsbeteiligung und Rechtsschutz nach dem Standortauswahlgesetz im Verhältnis zum atomrechtlichen Genehmigungsverfahren*, "NVwZ" 2014, p. 831.
118 D.Häfner, *The future* . . . , p. 42.
119 Factual composition was later subject of critique: A.Losada, D.Themann, M.Di Nucci, *Experts* . . . , pp. 250–251.
120 J.Schwabe, *Grundkurs Staatsrecht*, Berlin 1995, p. 23.
121 B.Schmidt-Bleibtreu [in:] B.Schmidt-Bleibtreu, F.Klein (eds.), *Kommentar zum Grundgesetz*, Berlin 1995, p. 494.
122 See FCC judgement of 15 February 1978, ref. 2 BvR 134, 268/76, publ. BVerfGE47,253, p. 273.
123 Cf. FCC judgement of 26 June 1990, ref. 2 BvF 3/89, publ. BVerfGE83,60, p. 73.
124 BVerfGE83,60, p. 73.
125 P.Kunig (ed.), *Grundgesetz-Kommentar. Band 1*, München 1992, p. 1054.
126 Ibid.
127 J.Schwabe, *Grundkurs* . . . , p. 23.
128 As of 11 June 2016.
129 See <www.bundestag.de/endlager/mitglieder/kommission>.
130 See M.Schüring, *"Bekennen gegen den Atomstaat". Historische und religiöse Codierungen im kirchlichen Protest gegen die Atomenergie in den 70er und 80er Jahren* [in:] J.Ostheimer, M.Vogt (reds.), *Die Moral der Energiewende. Risikowhrnehmung im Wandel m Beispiel der Atomenergie*, Stuttgart 2014, pp. 230–243. On the earlier involvement of the Evangelical Church see. G.Niemeier, *Evangelische Stimmen zur Atomfrage*, Hannover 1958, pp. 15–103.
131 M.Wiegand, *Konsens* . . . , p. 832.
132 See explanatory memorandum to the bill, p. 48.
133 M.Kloepfer, D.Bruch, *Die Laufzeitverlängerung im Atomrecht zwischen Gesetz und Vertrag*, "Juristen Zeitung" 2011, p. 377.
134 Ibid.
135 See explanatory memorandum to the bill, p. 46.
136 Ibid., p. 47.
137 M.Wiegand, *Konsens* . . . , p. 831.
138 Ibid.
139 J.Olliges, *A "Deliberative Turn"* . . . , p. 265.
140 M.Wiegand, *Konsens* . . . , p. 831. Some assessments that follow conclusion of HLRWD-Commission seem to confirm those predictions – see M.Di Nucci,

A.Brunnengräber, *Making nuclear waste problems governable. Conflicts, participation and acceptability* [in:] A.Brunnengräber, M.Di Nucci (eds.), *Conflicts, participation and acceptability in nuclear waste governance*, Wiesbaden 2019, p. 14; J.Olliges *A "Deliberative Turn"* . . . , p. 267 et seq.

141 M.Wiegand, *Konsens* . . . , p. 832.

142 Ibid.

143 Ibid.

144 See Explanatory memorandum to the *Standortauswahlgesetz* bill, p. 43.

145 That was the term used by 2013-*Standortauswahlgesetz*.

146 That was the term used by 2017-*Standortauswahlgesetz*.

147 See further M.Schreurs, J.Suckow, *Bringing transparency* . . . , pp. 301 et seq.

148 See HLRWD-Commission, *Abschlussbericht* . . .

149 M.Schreurs, J.Suckow, *Bringing transparency* . . . , p. 298.

150 Ibid., pp. 298–299. See also further on their methodology: S.Kanitz, *Safely stored for all eternity. How The Bundesgesellschaft für Endlagerung is conducting its search for a repository for high-level radioactive waste*, „atw. International Journal for Nuclear Power" 2020, vol. 6–7, p. 332 et seq.

151 M.Schreurs, J.Suckow, *Bringing transparency* . . . , p. 298.

152 Ibid.

153 Ibid., pp. 298–299.

154 Ibid., p. 299.

155 HLRWD-Commission, *Abschlussbericht* . . .

156 Ibid., p. 498 and 517.

157 Ibid., p. 517.

158 Information from the Bundestag press service: "Endlager-Kommission gibt Zeitplan auf", 2 June 2016. <www.bundestag.de/presse/hib/201606/-/425748>.

159 Ibid.

160 Ibid.

161 See J.Stonington, *Sticker shock: The soaring costs of Germany's nuclear shutdown*, "Yale Environment 360", 25 July 2016. <http://e360.yale.edu/features/soaring_cost_german_nuclear_shutdown>; HLRWD-Commission, *Abschlussbericht* . . . , p. 517; *Zeitplan zur Endlagerung laut Kommission unrealistisch* "ZEIT ONLINE", 2 June 2016. <www.zeit.de/wirtschaft/2016-06/atommuell-endlager-kommission-zeitbedarf>.

162 HLRWD-Commission, *Abschlussbericht* . . . , p. 35.

163 Ibid., p. 26 and 31.

164 Ibid., pp. 26–27 and 31.

165 A.Losada, D.Themann, M.Di Nucci, *Experts* . . . , p. 244.

166 HLRWD-Commission, *Abschlussbericht* . . . , p. 27.

167 Ibid., p. 31.

168 Ibid.

169 Ibid., p. 35.

170 Ibid., p. 33.

171 Ibid., p. 33 and 34.

172 Ibid., p. 34.

173 Ibid.

174 Ibid., p. 41.

175 Ibid., p. 42.

176 M.Wiegand, *Konsens* . . . , p. 835.

177 Ibid.

178 HLRWD-Commission, *Abschlussbericht . . .* , p. 46.
179 Ibid.
180 Ibid.
181 Ibid.
182 Ibid.
183 Ibid., p. 60.
184 Ibid., p. 495.
185 Ibid., p. 498 and pp. 514–515.
186 Ibid., pp. 498–499.
187 Ibid., p. 499 and 515.
188 Ibid., p. 499.
189 See M.Di Nucci, *Voluntarism in Siting Nuclear Waste Disposal Facilities* [in:] A.Brunnengräber, M.Di Nucci (eds.), *Conflicts . . .* , p. 148 et seq.
190 Ibid., pp. 167–168.
191 Ibid., pp. 497–498 and p. 520.
192 See A.Roβnagel, *Kurzgutachten Verankerung des Atomausstiegs im Grundgesetz*, Kassel 2016. <www.bundestag.de/blob/423522/d3058f11bea5ebff1f36bf09dd6eb7e7/kmat_62-data.pdf>; K.Gärditz, *Verankerung des Atomausstiegs im Grundgesetz? Gutachten für die Kommission Lagerung hoch radioaktiver Abfallstoffe vorgelegt am 29. März 2016.* <www.bundestag.de/blob/423518/abafd18de79f9806d1ce98f2f9053feb/kmat_61-data.pdf>.
193 HLRWD-Commission, *Abschlussbericht . . .* , pp. 65–64.

References

Becker P., *Aufstieg und Krise der deutschen Stromkonzerne*, Bochum 2011.

Blowers A., *The legacy of nuclear power and what should be done about it* [in:] A.Brunnengräber, M.Di Nucci (eds.), *Conflicts, participation and acceptability in nuclear waste governance*, Wiesbaden 2019.

Bohne E., Speyer M., *Staat und Konfliktbewältigung bei Zukunftstechnologien*, „Neue Zeitschrift für Verwaltungsrecht" 1999, pp. 1–11.

Brunnengräber A., *The wicked problem of long term radioactive waste governance* [in:] A.Brunnengräber, M.Di Nucci (eds.), *Conflicts, participation and acceptability in nuclear waste governance*, Wiesbaden 2019.

Bundesminister des Innern, *Antwort der Bundesregierung auf die Große Anfrage der Abgeordneten Dr. Laufs, Dr. Dregger, Spranger, Dr. Riesenhuber, Dr. Miltner, Lenzer, Broll, Fellner, Dr. von Geldern, Gerlach, Dr. Waffenschmidt, Dr. Bugl, Gerstein, Frau Hürland, Kolb, Dr. George, Dr. Jobst, Dr. Köhler (Wolfsburg), Dr. Kunz (Weiden), Magin, Pfeffermann, Prangenberg, Schwarz, Dr. Stavenhagen und der Fraktion der CDU/CSU – Drucksache 9/858 – Verantwortung des Bundes für Sicherstellung und Endlagerung radioaktiver Abfälle in der Bundesrepublik Deutschland* of 22 December 1981, „Deutscher Bundestag Drucksache 9/1231", pp. 1–14.

Däuper O., Bernstorff A., *Gesetz zur Suche und Auswahl eines Standortes für die Endlagerung radioaktiver Abfälle – zugleich ein Vorschlag für die Agenda der „Kommission Lagerung hoch radioaktiver Abfallstoffe"*, „ZUR" 2014, pp. 24–32.

Däuper O., Bosch K., Ringwald R., *Zur Finanzierung des Standortauswahlverfahrens für ein atomares Endlager durch Beiträge der Abfallverursacher*, „ZUR" 2013, pp. 329–336.

Deutscher Depeschendienst, *Interview: Endlager Gorleben aus Expertensicht nur zweite Wahl.* www.verivox.de/nachrichten/interview-endlager-gorleben-aus-expertensicht-nur-zweite-wahl-43384/.

Di Nucci M., *Voluntarism in siting nuclear waste disposal facilities* [in:] A.Brunnengräber, M.Di Nucci (eds.), *Conflicts, participation and acceptability in nuclear waste governance*, Wiesbaden 2019.

Drögemüller C., *Schlüsselakteure der Endlager-Governance. Entsorgungsoptionen und – strategien radioaktiver Abfälle aus Sicht regionaler Akteure*, Wiesbaden 2018.

Gärditz K., *Verankerung des Atomausstiegs im Grundgesetz? Gutachten für die Kommission Lagerung hoch radioaktiver Abfallstoffe vorgelegt am 29. März 2016.* www.bundestag.de/blob/423518/abafd18de79f9806d1ce98f2f9053feb/kmat_61-data.pdf.

Häfner D., *The future is still unwritten – history too. Overcoming the conflicts of the past in Germany* [in:] A.Brunnengräber, M.Di Nucci (eds.), *Conflicts, participation and acceptability in nuclear waste governance*, Wiesbaden 2019.

Hocke P., Brunnengräber A., *Multi-level governance of nuclear waste disposal* [in:] A.Brunnengräber, M.Di Nucci (eds.), *Conflicts, participation and acceptability in nuclear waste governance*, Wiesbaden 2019.

Kamlage J., Warode J., Mengede A., *Chances, challenges and choices of participation in siting a nuclear waste repository* [in:] A.Brunnengräber, M.Di Nucci (eds.), *Conflicts, participation and acceptability in nuclear waste governance*, Wiesbaden 2019.

Kanitz S., *Safely stored for all eternity. How the Bundesgesellschaft für Endlagerung is conducting its search for a repository for high-level radioactive waste*, „atw. International Journal for Nuclear Power" 2020, vol. 6–7, pp. 331–333.

Kirchhof A., Trischler H., *The history behind West Germany's nuclear phase-out* [in:] *A. Kirchhof pathways into and out of nuclear power in Western Europe Austria, Denmark, Federal Republic of Germany, Italy, and Sweden*, Munich 2020.

Kloepfer M., Bruch D., *Die Laufzeitverlängerung im Atomrecht zwischen Gesetz und Vertrag*, „Juristen Zeitung" 2011, pp. 377–387.

Koch H., Roβnagel A., *Neue Energiepolitik und Ausstieg aus der Kernenergie*, „NVwZ" 2000, p. 1 et seq.

Kommission Lagerung hoch radioaktiver Abfallstoffe, *Abschlussbericht. Verantwortung für die Zukunft. Ein faires und transparentes Verfahren für die Auswahl eines nationalen Endlagerstandortes*, Berlin 2016. www.bundestag.de/endlager-archiv/blob/434430/bb37b21b8e1e7e049ace5db6b2f949b2/drs_268-data.pdf.

Kunig P. (ed.), *Grundgesetz-Kommentar. Band 1*, München 1992.

Losada A., Themann D., Di Nucci M., *Experts and politics in the German nuclear waste governance* [in:] A.Brunnengräber, M.Di Nucci (eds.), *Conflicts, participation and acceptability in nuclear waste governance*, Wiesbaden 2019.

Niemeier G., *Evangelische Stimmen zur Atomfrage*, Hannover 1958.

Niewodniczański J., *Wprowadzenie do energetyki jądrowej* [in:] K.Jeleń, Z.Rau (eds.), *Energetyka jądrowa w Polsce*, Warszawa 2012.

Nucci Di M., Brunnengräber, A., *Making nuclear waste problems governable. Conflicts, participation and acceptability* [in:] A.Brunnengräber, M.Di Nucci (eds.), *Conflicts, participation and acceptability in nuclear waste governance*, Wiesbaden 2019.

Offermann C., *Die Entsorgung radioaktiver Abfälle eine Stellungnahme zum Entsorgungsbericht'88*, "NVwZ" 1989, pp. 1112–1120.

Olliges J., *A "deliberative turn" in German nuclear waste governance?* [in:] A.Brunnengräber, M.Di Nucci (eds.), *Conflicts, participation and acceptability in nuclear waste governance*, Wiesbaden 2019.

Ramana M., *Why technical solutions are insufficient. The abiding conundrum of nuclear waste* [in:] A.Brunnengräber, M.Di Nucci (eds.), *Conflicts, participation and acceptability in nuclear waste governance*, Wiesbaden 2019.

Roβnagel A., *Kurzgutachten Verankerung des Atomausstiegs im Grundgesetz*, Kassel 2016. www.bundestag.de/blob/423522/d3058f11bea5ebff1f36bf09dd6eb7e7/kmat_62-data.pdf.

Röhlig K., *The ENTRIA Project (2013–2018)* [in:] A.Brunnengräber, M.Di Nucci (eds.), *Conflicts, participation and acceptability in nuclear waste governance*, Wiesbaden 2019.

Rybski R., *Judgment of the Federal Constitutional Court of 17 December 2013. (ref: 1 BvR 3139/08, 1 BvR 3386/08) on energy security as a premise allowing expropriation for the purpose of constructing an open-pit lignite mine*, "Przegląd Sejmowy" 2015, No. 5.

Schmidt-Bleibtreu B., Klein F., *Kommentar zum Grundgesetz*, Berlin 1995.

Schreurs M., Suckow J., *Bringing transparency and voice into the search for a deep geological repository. Nuclear waste governance in Germany and the Role of the National Civil Society Board – Nationales Begleitgremium (NBG)* [in:] A.Brunnengräber, M.Di Nucci (eds.), *Conflicts, participation and acceptability in nuclear waste governance*, Wiesbaden 2019.

Schüring M., *„Bekennen gegen den Atomstaat". Historische und religiöse Codierungen im kirchlichen Protest gegen die Atomenergie in den 70er und 80er Jahren* [in:] J.Ostheimer, M.Vogt (eds.), *Die Moral der Energiewende. Risikowahrnehmung im Wandel m Beispiel der Atomenergie*, Stuttgart 2014.

Schwabe J., *Grundkurs Staatsrecht*, Berlin 1995.

Stonington J., *Sticker Shock: The Soaring Costs of Germany's Nuclear Shutdown*, "Yale Environment 360", 25 July 2016. http://e360.yale.edu/features/soaring_cost_german_nuclear_shutdown.

Tiggemann A., *The elephant in the room. The role of Gorleben and its site selection in the German nuclear waste debate* [in:] A.Brunnengräber, M.Di Nucci (eds.), *Conflicts, participation and acceptability in nuclear waste governance*, Wiesbaden 2019.

Tiggemann A., *Gorleben – Entsorgungsstandort auf der Grundlage eines sachgerechten Auswahlverfahrens*, „Atomwirtschaft" 2010, vol. 10, pp. 606–615.

Tiggemann A., *Der niedersächsische Auswahl- und Entscheidungsprozess. Expertise zur Standortauswahl für das „Entsorgungszentrum" 1976/77*, Hannover 2010, p. 79. www.umwelt.niedersachsen.de/download/35842.

Übereinkommen über nukleare Sicherheit. Bericht der Bundesrepublik Deutschland für die Achte Überprüfungstagung im März/April 2020, Bonn 2019.

Übereinkommen über nukleare Sicherheit. Bericht der Bundesrepublik Deutschland für die Sechste Überprüfungstagung im März/April 2014, Bonn 2013.

Wiegand M., *Konsens durch Verfahren? Öffentlichkeitsbeteiligung und Rechtsschutz nach dem Standortauswahlgesetz im Verhältnis zum atomrechtlichen Genehmigungsverfahren*, „NVwZ" 2014, pp. 830–835.

Wolltenteit U., *Gorleben und kein Ende*, „ZUR" 2014, pp. 323–329.

Zeitplan zur Endlagerung laut Kommission unrealistisch, "ZEIT ONLINE", 2 June 2016. www.zeit.de/wirtschaft/2016-06/atommuell-endlager-kommission-zeitbedarf.

4 Concluding remarks

Both the provisions of *Grundgesetz* and the FCC's case law presented, which deal with the peaceful use of nuclear energy, provide valuable insight. It is possible to recommend the application of convergent constitutional provisions and standards resulting from the FCC case law in other democratic countries functioning on the basis of the rule of law. The appropriateness of the application of the acquis resulting from the German legal system and the case law of the German Constitutional Court applies equally to countries that are about to start using nuclear energy for electricity generation (such as Poland), are already using it (such as France) or are considering a nuclear phase-out. The adequacy of solutions and standards stemming from the German legal system is due to the fact that the political system of the Federal Republic of Germany was adjusted to the nuclear power industry even before the establishment of commercial nuclear power plants, and subsequently key decisions were made in the legislative procedure (e.g. on nuclear phase-out or disposal of radioactive waste). In addition, there is a wealth of case law on the subject, as well as numerous documents on various aspects of nuclear power available in the literature. The appropriateness of using Germany's wealth of experience with nuclear power within other constitutional systems is evidenced by the fact, among other things, that the subsequent statutory changes were not theoretical, but had a real impact on one of the world's largest economies. At its peak, nuclear power provided nearly 30% of Germany's electricity needs. The combined actions of the legislature, the executive branch, and the judiciary have had (and continue to have) a real impact on gigantic assets that have significantly contributed to the energy security of one of the world's most industrialised countries.

The decisive voice of the social side means that by engaging in the work of the HLRWD-Commission, it took co-responsibility for the solutions worked out. In turn, the representatives of the Bundestag who have been involved in the work of the HLRWD-Commission at all times will not be able to disregard the HLRWD-Commission's findings either. In fact, this applies to the entire Bundestag,

DOI: 10.4324/9781003198086-5

since members of Parliament represent their parliamentary clubs when they work in the Commission. Thus, the engagement mechanism provided by the Act is a thoughtful solution that provided an opportunity to develop appropriate outcomes, i.e. compromise between the various parties to the dispute. At the same time, it is a self-learning process, that already four years after its adoption underwent heavy changes.

Appendix 1

Contents of Exhibit 4 to the contract dated 14 June 2000 between the Federal Government and the energy companies:

> "Federation statement on Gorleben salt deposit exploration
>
> Under Section 9a(3) of the Federal Atomic Law, the Federation has a statutory responsibility to establish a [nuclear] disposal facility for radioactive waste. The Federal Government affirms that it has this responsibility and declares that it will take the necessary measures to prepare the radioactive waste final disposal facility of adequate capacity in time, in a manner that will not result in the abandonment of nuclear energy.
>
> Both salt deposits and other types of geological deposits, such as granite or clay, are being considered as possible geological formations for the radioactive waste final disposal facility. The geological information obtained so far is as follows: the dimensions and expansion of the old rock salt deposits, which were previously thought to be suitable for the storage of high-level radioactive waste, turned out to be larger than initially assumed following the survey work [. . .]. For this reason, the area surveyed to date is not sufficient for the anticipated amount of waste.
>
> The rate of uplift of the salt deposits, as determined after the survey work, allows us to expect that these deposits are not expected to be uplifted in the very long time horizon (about one million years) either. No significant gas formations, condensates, or dissolution were discovered in the old rock salt deposits. The existing survey [of the Gorleben rock salt deposits] confirms the presence of thick [rock salt] deposits which will provide a suitable protective barrier through the [layer of] salt. Therefore, the geological data collected to date do not call into question the suitability of the Gorleben salt seams [to serve as a final disposal facility for radioactive waste].

Admittedly, in view of the ongoing international discussion on the need to expand the basic requirements for radioactive waste final disposal facilities, the Federal Government will continue to develop and refine the concept of the radioactive waste disposal facility. The state of the art and technology, as well as the overall risk assessment have developed considerably in recent years; this has a corresponding impact on the exploitation of the salt seams in Gorleben.

The following issues in particular are still in doubt:

- a particular problem is [the development of knowledge and technology so that there is] the control of gas generation in deep salt seams due to corrosion and decay of radioactive waste;
- there is an increasingly strong voice in international discussions regarding the need to maintain the [technical] capability [to design and construct the radioactive waste final disposal facility in terms of] of bringing radioactive waste back [to the surface] in the future. The concept so far, on the other hand, is to seal [irreversibly] [radioactive waste in deposits of] salt;
- the use of rock salt seams as rock deposits [in which the radioactive waste final disposal facility will be placed] should be compared with [deposits] such as clay or granite, and studied, based on experience in other countries;
- during direct final disposal [of radioactive waste], spent fuel must meet additional requirements to be able to preclude in the long term [spontaneous] transition to a critical state (critical accumulation of fissile material [resulting in spontaneous initiation of the fission process and uncontrolled generation of energy]).
- soon, the International Commission on Radiation Protection will probably present an opinion that for the first time formulates objectives for radiological protection in the event of unintentional human intrusion into a final disposal facility [of radioactive waste].

Further exploration of the Gorleben salt deposits will not resolve the issues mentioned. For this reason, [further] exploitation of the salt beds in Gorleben will be discontinued for at least three years and for a maximum of ten years; [at the same time] clarifications of the previously mentioned issues will be worked out as soon as possible.

The moratorium does not mean abandoning Gorleben as the location of a [radioactive waste] disposal facility. On the contrary, its purpose is that in the course of answering questions about the design and safety of [a future radioactive waste final disposal facility], no project will be made that will not lead to clarification of these issues.

The Federation will take the necessary measures to protect the Gorleben site during the moratorium period. This involves all necessary legal actions to maintain the Federation's position as applicant and to protect [the Gorleben site] from interference by third parties. The Federation will take the necessary steps to obtain a ten-year extension of the validity of the mine plan for the rock formation [at Gorleben site] [. . .]".[1]

Note

1 Translation based on the agreement available in: P.Becker, *Aufstieg und Krise der deutschen Stromkonzerne*, Bochum 2011, pp. 359–360.

Index

For Product Safety Concerns and Information please contact our EU representative GPSR@taylorandfrancis.com Taylor & Francis Verlag GmbH, Kaufingerstraße 24, 80331 München, Germany

Printed and bound by CPI Group (UK) Ltd, Croydon, CR0 4YY

11/04/2025

01844012-0005